WONDERFUL

WEARABLES

BAZAAR BIRDS AND BEASTS: award-winning jacket by the author of handwoven Guatemalan cotton. Silk, cotton and lamé applique embellished with hand and machine embroidery, beads and shi-shas. Fasteners are muñecas, Guatemalan folk dolls. Made for Bazaar del Mundo fashion fair.

WONDERFUL WEARABLES

A Celebration of Creative Clothing

By Virginia Avery

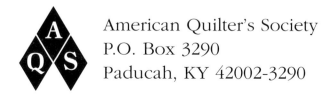

American Quilter's Society
P.O. Box 3290
Paducah, KY 42002-3290

Library of Congress
Cataloging-in-Publication Data
Avery, Virginia.
Wonderful Wearables: A Celebration of Creative Clothing / by Virginia Avery.
p. cm.
Includes index.
ISBN 0-89145-980-4: $24.95
1. Clothing and dress. I. Title.
TT519.5.A84   1991
746.9'2–dc20   91-31157 CIP

Additional copies of this book may be ordered from:

American Quilter's Society
P.O. Box 3290
Paducah, KY 42002-3290

@$24.95. Add $1.00 for postage & handling.

Table of Contents

WITHOUT FURTHER ADO…

Ever since I was a little girl, I've loved clothes and I've loved to sew. I scrounged scraps when I was five to make a wardrobe for my doll, and I made my first dress when I was 12 because I was afraid if I didn't my mother would. Mother's idea of high style for a 12 year old girl was a print dress with a drawstring neck and drawstring waist; she used both in a dress for me and sent me off to school. All day I was taunted with "yah, yah, yah! Tied up in a sack!" – this of course from the boys, testing their mettle. The girls wouldn't have dared. I never wore that dress again, and I never told my mother why. From then on, I took responsibility for my wardrobe, such as it was, and I think Mother was secretly relieved.

I taught myself to sew on her old treadle machine. There were lots of trials and errors. Often, I cut into fabric without benefit of a pattern, (I know better now), and I remember making one dress which did not meet in the front by six or seven inches. Undaunted, I set in a panel of contrasting fabric and was careful to let everyone know I had done it deliberately; retrieving a potential disaster was a challenge and a triumph for me, and it still is.

When I was in high school, my favorite uncle brought me a silk Japanese kimono, a real one. I had never seen anything like it before, and I hardly knew where Japan was on the map. The kimono set my mind whirling. I loved the swirling design and the sensuous feel of the silk. When I wore it, I felt absolutely magical. That kimono was special in so many ways – a gift from one of my favorite people, a mysterious, elegant garment that evoked a romantic and exotic land, and – although I did not recognize it at the time – it was my introduction to ethnic clothes. These are the easy, comfortable and beautifully simple garments of other worlds, other cultures, and they fit amazingly into our own lives. Inspired by them, we can create unique and lasting garments for ourselves.

These clothes, although dictated by function, generate a beauty and simplicity far beyond necessity. The styles, the handwork, the embel-lishments and embroidery all are imbued with a meaning far beyond surface design. Such clothes are identification, communication and spiritual food.

I sewed through college and afterward created my working wardrobes for the jobs I had. After I married and was raising a family, I taught sewing in nearby fabric shops. I also tried custom millinery and loved it – you could do *anything* with hats and get away with it. Then women stopped wearing hats, which promptly put me out of business. I learned stitchery and embroidery and realized early on that a big vocabulary of stitches was not essential; six or seven of the basic ones continue to serve me well.

My kids grew up, and in the 1960's I noticed two things happening which were of interest to me. First, the "flower children" and the "hippies" of the West Coast were rebelling against conventional clothes and wearing outrageous but creative outfits they made themselves. The second thing I noticed was that quilts were "coming back." Quilts were not new to me; I had a number of family quilts, and my grandmother made many applique quilts. I had always taken them for granted, but suddenly I saw them in a new light, a new direction for needle and thread and fabric, and I taught myself to quilt. When I thought I was good enough, I began to teach it to others, and I was amazed at the interest shown; women were hungry to learn. The Bicentennial was also in the wings, and I watched many Bicentennial quilts come to life. Most of these were pictorial applique, and the interest in applique spread to other areas, too. All of this led, of course, to THE BIG BOOK OF APPLIQUE, which Scribners published for me in 1978. With the Bicentennial, and the Whitney Museum exhibit of quilts in 1971, quilting became firmly established as part of our daily routine.

The clothing revolution of the 1960's led to the Wearable Art movement of the 1970's which is still with us and thriving; it has been through ups and downs, but it's still here. It affirms the creativity of women – and men, too – who have something to say and want to wear their statements.

Arriving early on the quilting scene helped me in many ways. I've been fortunate in teaching at quilt conferences since their inception. The first was held in 1976, and since then, they have multiplied like rabbits. The conference was a novel idea. It brought quilters and would-be quilters together in a central place for a few days of concentrated workshops and lectures. It spawned shops and vendors, books and magazines, a show-and-tell session, and it spawned fashion shows. Even then, women were making simple patchwork clothing, and the strip-pieced vest or log cabin jacket became de rigueur. Skirts were decorated with quilt-block borders around the hemlines. Women wore these at conferences, displayed them at show-and-tell, and modeled them in the fashion shows; it became quite clear that patchwork clothing, as well as quilted clothing, was an extension of quiltmaking, and this led to my book *Quilts To Wear*. Scribners published it in 1982; it was, and still is, a definitive book on quilted clothing. Making such garments is enormously satisfying; you wear your art, and you get instant strokes.

Quilt conferences today have multiplied to dizzying figures; there are more scheduled than it is possible to attend. One of the most important conference events is the fashion show, and it has become almost as popular as the quilt exhibit. The Fairfield-Concord Fashion Show, which debuts every year at the Houston Quilt Market and Festival, is the biggest and best known. Thousands see this show, and it travels for a year, not only throughout the United States, but abroad as well. Each entry is an outward expression of inner creative drive, a joyous testimony to the makers. The American Quilter's Society also sponsors a fashion show for their annual conference, and galleries all over the country are sponsoring creative clothing exhibits.

Nothing ever stands still or stays the same. In quilting we have seen remarkable changes – stunning innovations and experiments as quilters stretch themselves and their imaginations to embrace new concepts. Women do the same when they are creating special garments; my classes are filled with women excited over the prospects of making something unique which they can wear. Their garments must enhance their personalities, and convey to the world the pride they have in their own accomplishments. There have been, and are, new approaches to design and color, new ways of doing things – refinements perhaps, on old techniques. Creative clothing has paralleled the advance in quiltmaking.

I've thought about these changes for a long time, wanting to put them in another book, and I couldn't help but be reminded of the play *Amadeus*. Young Mozart was commissioned by the King to write a piece of music. After a time, the King asked if he had finished it. Mozart said that yes, indeed he had. "Well," said the King, "where is it?" Amadeus tapped his head. "In here. I have only to transfer it to paper." This book has been up there in my head for the past couple of years, trying to get out, and finally, it has.

As you know, there are lots of "Joys" in book titles – *The Joy of Cooking*, *The Joy of Sex*, *The Joy of Aerobics*, *The Joy of Running* and so on. I could have called this book *The Joy of Creating Your Own Clothes* or *The Joy of Wearable Art*. I could also have called it *Daughter of Quilts to Wear*, but I caught myself just in time. The book is all about wonderful wearables, and that's what it's called: *Wonderful Wearables*. It's a celebration of creative clothing.

These pages are filled with ideas and inspiration for you. You'll be encouraged to develop your sense of color and design, to try new fabric combinations and let yourself go with embellishments. The sewing is simple. It has to be. All of us in today's society are desperate for time; there is never enough, but you still have to hang on to some for yourself. You're a priority, too. The special garments you make for yourself are timeless. They aren't "in" this year and "out" the next. They're "forever" clothes, always in style, and they have heirloom possibilities, whether simple or elaborate, whimsical or elegant. They'll tell the world who you are and how you want to be seen by others.

I hope someday we can have a class together, but until then, go with this book.

"Of Thee I Sing, Baby," worn as a cape. Painted, pieced, appliqued, quilted, embellished, written on and rubber stamped. By the author.

PATTERNS:
Simple shapes, super style

The care and feeding of the imagination is a life-long process, a nurturing one. We are constantly looking for anything which will "spark" our imaginations and set them in motion; sometimes it's such a little thing we don't recognize it.

Many times women come into my classes, their arms bulging with stacks of fabric and other supplies. They put the stuff down on the table and say, "I really don't know why I came; I don't have any ideas at all. I don't have the slightest idea of what I want to make."

What they don't realize is that they have already started wheels turning with their fabric selection. They didn't just happen to have those particular fabrics – they went out and bought them because they liked them. They liked the color, the pattern, or both, as well as the texture. This is a good beginning. Sometimes beginnings are very hard. It helps to first narrow your choices. Do you want a coat, a jacket, a vest, a cape or another type of garment? Do you want it for general use or a special event? Will it be worn inside or out? In summer or winter, or does it matter? How much time and effort can you spend on it? Answering these questions will help you zero in on your project.

Design and inspiration are all around us, but we have to be aware of them. We have to sharpen our senses and train our eyes to see and our ears to hear, for things which passed unnoticed before might be the very ones to turn us on now. Fashion magazines and books can inspire; they are filled with ideas from the fashion world, enough to start the juices flowing. Street fashion helps, and so do window displays. If something really catches your eye, go into the store and take a closer look. Written words help to inspire also, for they conjure up images for you. Newspaper ads, magazine ads or graphic displays may have an impact, too. There's no substitute for observation; Michaelangelo was obsessed with this. He called it "saper videre," learning or knowing how to see, and he trained himself constantly to be alert. Books on the history of costume offer worlds of information, and so do the costume departments of museums. Libraries are filled with resource materials, and you can pack yourself so full of ideas you may not know how to pick and choose. I carry a notebook with me, and when I see or hear something I want to remember, I make a note of it. I also do rough sketches – and believe me, they really are rough! They serve the purpose though: they jog the memory later.

When you decide to make a Wonderful Wearable for yourself, I hope you remember that fashion is fleeting. Don't be swept away with current styles – they may be past history tomorrow. Think back over some of the fashion flurries and you'll know what I mean. Coats and jackets are loose and full one year, fitted the next. Hems are up, hems are down. Pants are full, pants are tapered at the ankle. Dresses are tailored, dresses are feminine and frothy. Red is out, purple is in. High heels for evening, flats for day, and so on endlessly. If you wait long enough too, old style will be popular again and couture designers will try to convince you that they alone have developed it. There are two designers, for my money, who should be honored forever. Poiret emancipated women from corsets, and Chanel put women in pants. To me, these make up for a lot – even what the designers did to women and their bosoms. Remember? They squeezed them together, pushed them up, separated them, mashed them flat, rounded them off, pointed them upward, padded, draped and sometimes bared them. Poiret and Chanel evened the score.

One of the little design gimmicks I find very helpful, and one I use in my classes, is what I call the "open window" to design. These are cutout shapes and they can help you with pattern and color. On pages 158-159 you will find six rather basic garment shapes. Trace them to lightweight cardboard or an old manila folder; then, with a craft knife, cut out the marked areas. Now use colored ads or photos from a magazine. I use *Vogue* or some of the other fashion magazines, and I also use *National Geographic*. Lay

USING BASIC GARMENT CUTOUTS FOR DESIGN IDEAS

Six full-size basic garment cutouts for "open window" designing are found in the pattern section on pages 158-159.

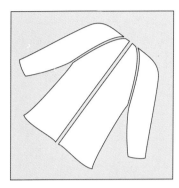

"Of Thee I Sing, Baby," a half-circle cape/coat designed and made by the author. Shown here hanging on wall when not being worn.

Bog Coat variation with extended sleeve and front closing. Designed and made by the author.

Front view of zebra "terrific tunic vest" by the author. Inspired by the sequin zebra (upper left shoulder), a gift from Marinda Stewart. Pieced silk, cotton and ribbon, buttons added.

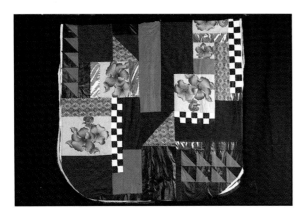

Back view of "Passion," a poncho by Barbara Smith-Huggins.

the cutout over the page, and before your eyes you'll see design take shape. Ideas about color and placement will spring to life. Move the cutout around to various places on the page, for "a change of scenery." Try it on newspaper ads for a graphic shape in black and white. My classes are very enthusiastic about this "open window" method and I know that you will be too.

Design isn't always easy. You can't turn it on like a faucet, but, as I have pointed out, there are ways to get started. Once you have an idea you can work out the details. Sometimes it takes an idea a long time to come together for me; I call it the incubation period. An idea may churn around in my mind for some time before I'm ready for it, and even then, after I've started a project, it may change halfway through. Ideas often have a life of their own.

PATTERNS

Paper patterns originated in France in medieval times, when Europe had its early contacts with the Orient and fashionable clothes became very important. At first, only tailors were allowed to use the patterns, crude as they were, but some 400 years later Louis XIV finally gave permission to dressmakers to use the patterns for their customers – usually wealthy women who enjoyed the court society. These patterns were a confusing maze of lines, with all sections of the garment superimposed on one sheet of paper. We can be thankful patterns have finally evolved into the clear-cut, simple and workable ones we have now. Each section of today's patterns is marked with both seam and cutting lines and notches for matching. Each pattern also has detailed instructions on cutting, fitting and sewing – a road map to success.

There are two major categories of patterns on the market. The first is ethnic. These patterns are simple in shape, for they were designed originally for cloth just off the loom, with no darts and a minimum of cutting and sewing. Folkwear Patterns is the largest ethnic pattern company, and their designs are quite authentic, patterned after clothing worn in different countries, for different events, for different social or tribal celebrations. Folkwear Patterns is now owned by the Taunton Press, the people who publish *Threads* magazine. Yvonne Porcella has also published four small pattern books. *Pieced Clothing* and *Pieced Clothing Variations* are the best known and are still available. They are not full-size patterns as are Folkwear; these are diagrams, much the same as are in this book, and by following the measurements and instructions, you make your own full-sized pattern. Marit Kucera has a few patterns out, a cocoon jacket for one. Ethnic patterns by others appear from time to time. The vending area of any quilt conference or exhibit is a good place to look for them; many are also sold by mail order through quilt catalogs.

These ethnic, or simple, styles are geometric wonders. They are based on squares or rectangles, triangles and circles. None of them have darts, and this makes everything easier, for you can plan and develop your design on a flat surface. When you finish, you sew it up; the sewing is easy and fast, for the styles are uncomplicated. We use many ethnic designs in my classes because of their simplicity. Sometimes I teach a class where everyone works with the same pattern; then small miracles happen. No two garments are ever alike, for each one is a reflection of the person who made it, different in color and design and fabric. Most of these garments fit the body loosely, so there is little if any alteration or fitting to be done.

The second category is commercial patterns. These are produced by several companies; Vogue-Butterick, McCall's and Simplicity are the largest, oldest and best established, but a number of newcomers are creeping successfully into the ring. Burda, Style and New Look have all made an impact, and by the time you read this there may be others. These patterns are drafted according to a set of government measurements, although how the government set standards for women's shapes is more than I know. You usually buy the same size in a pattern as you would use in a ready-made purchased dress or other garment. I have noticed that in the past couple of years, pattern companies have started printing multi-size patterns, which means you get more for

"Bog Coat Goes to a Party," designed and made by the author for the 1991 Fairfield-Concord Fashion Show. Gray Facile®, bound with hand-dyed fabric. Buttonhole pockets and extended sleeves. Photo courtesy of Fairfield Processing Corp.

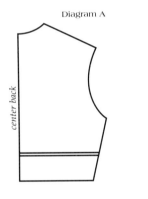

Back view of "Memories" vest by Margot Carter Blair. Chinese bookmarks on back are faced, then stitched only at top and bottom so they remain free. Made for Pacific Friendship Fiber Conference.

BASIC ALTERATIONS

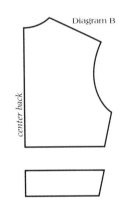

Diagram A   Diagram B

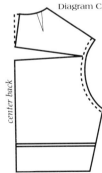

Diagram C

Diagram A is bodice back; the double horizontal lines are alteration lines. If bodice is too long, take a tuck on these lines. *Diagram B* is bodice back and shows alteration for lengthening. Cut pattern apart on alteration lines and insert tissue. *Diagram C* shows alteration for round shoulders. Slash across pattern back to seamline; spread pattern, add tissue. Straighten center back line to neck. The excess fabric caused by the slash will be taken up with a neck dart.

your money in case your top and bottom don't match up. In sized patterns, there is a 2" difference in the grading, so if you think you fall between two sizes – say between a 12 and a 14, purchase the smaller size. It is easier to make a pattern larger than the other way around.

On the back of the pattern envelope there usually is a chart of body measurements and you are supposed to compare your own to these. Several years ago, Vogue Pattern Company said there were 17 figure shapes to each size, and this only proves that we are fearfully and wonderfully made. It also proves that you had better check the fit of the pattern before you start your garment. You may need to do some fine-tuning.

I want to mention a few of the more obvious differences. Women, as you know, come in all sizes and shapes; tall or short, thin or well-padded, big busted or flat, broad shouldered or narrow, wide-hipped or not. Compare your own measurements with those of the pattern and make changes accordingly. Most women are familiar with the horizontal measurements, but not so well acquainted with the vertical ones. These have to do with whether you are long- or short-waisted, and whether your arms are longer or shorter than the pattern. There are instructions for these simple alterations in the pattern; for instance, if your waistline is longer than the pattern indicates, you cut the pattern along the alteration line and add a piece of tissue. If your measurement is less, you take a tuck in the pattern. The same type of alteration applies to arms; you check the length from shoulder to elbow, and from elbow to wrist. The alteration lines are double lines across the inside of the pattern piece. If you need serious alterations, there are some excellent books which can help. All the pattern companies, or most of them, have such books in print.

After you've altered your paper pattern, absolutely the best thing you can do for yourself is to make a "muslin." Cut the basic pieces from muslin or sheeting or some ugly fabric you have lying around, machine baste the garment together and try it on. Move in it, stretch in it and look at yourself in the mirror. Be sure that in cutting you have followed the grain line markings. If you're satisfied with the muslin, you're O.K. to go ahead. Otherwise, make the additional changes necessary. This muslin, or trial garment, is an insurance policy which really pays off.

I mentioned darts a little earlier: when you are working with patchwork clothes, it's easier to work flat than with darts. If, however, your figure is such that you think you need darts for better fit, try to choose a pattern with princess lines rather than a bust dart: a gored skirt rather than one with hip darts. The dart will be there, all right, but it will be concealed in the style line and will be much easier to sew.

You have a bigger choice of sleeves in a commercial or western pattern than you do in an ethnic one, and this may influence your choice. It is also possible to change sleeves without too much trouble, and sometimes they are even interchangeable with other patterns.

A set-in sleeve is a classic one, used primarily for tailored garments. It can be either one or two pieces, and is set into the armscye (armhole) at the shoulder line.

A raglan sleeve is a little sportier. It doesn't stop at the shoulder line, but is set in starting at the neck. It

BASIC SLEEVE ALTERATIONS

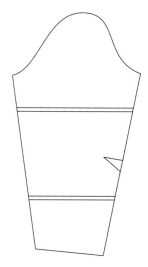

After measuring from top of sleeve to elbow, and from your elbow to wrist, compare to paper pattern. Make alterations on horizontal alteration lines found in both areas of sleeve pattern.

Tuck or fold to shorten; slash and add tissue to lengthen.

SET-IN SLEEVES

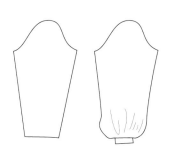

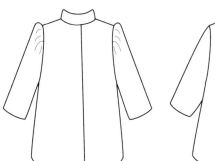

LEFT: A classic set-in sleeve. RIGHT: Set-in sleeve gathered into cuff.

LEFT: Coat with set-in sleeves, fullness gathered into sleeve seam at shoulder. CENTER: Coat with set-in sleeves and side closing. RIGHT: Coat with set-in sleeves and zigzag closing.

can also be one or two pieces. A one-piece raglan sleeve will have a dart at the top, starting at the neckline; the two-piece sleeve will have the dart incorporated into the seam, which runs from neck to wrist along the top of the arm.

A kimono sleeve (not to be confused with the

RAGLAN SLEEVE

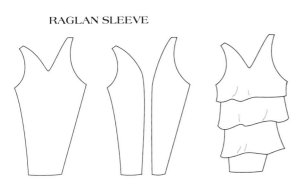

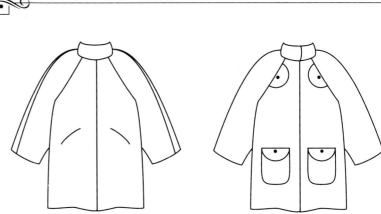

LEFT: A raglan sleeve. Dart gives fit to shoulder. CENTER: Two-piece raglan sleeve. Dart control incorporated in seam. RIGHT: Raglan sleeve with tiers of fabric for a different look.

LEFT: Raglan sleeve jacket with slot or buttonhole pockets. Two piece sleeve. RIGHT: Raglan sleeve jacket with buttoned tabs.

KIMONO-TYPE & SQUARE-CUT SLEEVE

LEFT: A kimono-type sleeve, cut in one with body of coat. RIGHT: Coat with square-cut sleeve.

SQUARE-CUT SLEEVE

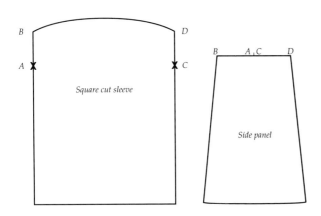

A square-cut sleeve. Sleeve and side panel are constructed as a unit. Stitch underarm sleeve seam from wrist to X marks. Then match remaining AB and CD to AB and CD of top edge of side panel. Stitch. This permits one long straight easy seam which attaches sleeve/side panel to the front and back units of the coat or jacket.

sleeve of a Japanese kimono), is cut as one piece with the bodice or body of the garment. There is a center back seam with this type of sleeve. If the sleeve is very wide underarm, it is sometimes called a dolman or bat-wing sleeve.

The dropped shoulder sleeve and the square-cut sleeve really belong to the ethnic group, but the commercial pattern companies have adopted them for many of their garments.

The diagrams at left show you how to sew a square-cut sleeve, and there also are instructions in the patterns. These sleeves are first stitched to side panels, then joined to the front and back of the garment in one long seam; the actual construction is very simple. Most ethnic sleeve patterns are fairly loose and wide, and you can change them easily if you like. Gather the bottom edge into a cuff or band; cut the sleeve wider so you can pleat or gather the top. You may substitute binding or lapels for straight neck bands, and you may add collars, pockets or belts.

When you want to use a commercial pattern for a patchwork or quilted garment, look for simple lines. I've given you a few guidelines on sleeves and these will help you in choosing. Study the pattern you like and choose one with a good cut. If there are unnecessary seams, eliminate them. Most of the time you can also eliminate facings, unless you are making an unlined garment. Some patterns have a great many pieces and are quite complicated; avoid these. Remember, the design you create will be easier and faster to do without unnecessary details.

SIMPLE SHAPES, SUPER STYLE

The really simple shapes, the geometric marvels, are a busy woman's answer to her wardrobe needs. They are almost accessories, for they complete the look of an outfit; they can be adapted for almost any occasion and take only a minimum of time to construct. Such shapes have ethnic origins and are found in almost all cultures; they vary in color and fiber and decoration, but basically they are the same. They may evoke strange and mysterious lands and customs, but they fit easily into a modern lifestyle.

PONCHOS AND CAPES

"Poncho" is a Spanish word, yet the garment itself probably originated in Peru. Today it is universal, known as a cape, a fling, a sweep, even a stole. It can be square or rectangular or circular with a hole for the head. It may be hip, ankle or mid-calf length, and opened down the front. The sides may be loose or they can be fastened together to form a type of sleeve. They are made of tweed or flannel for colder weather, of linen or cotton for warm weather, of silk or chiffon for evening. I often travel with a poncho; I not only wear it, but it also serves as an extra blanket on a chilly night and, rolled up, it becomes a pillow.

The easiest poncho to make is a square with a hole in the center. The hole is usually oval rather than round; if the oval is cut along the horizontal line or fold, the garment will be squared off in front and back. If the opening is cut along the diagonal fold, points of the square will be centered in front and back and over the arms.

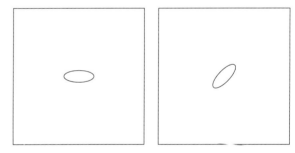

MEXICAN QUEXQUEMITL
A snug little shoulder poncho with a deep V neck. Make it out of two rectangles, 12" x 28"; fringe the ends. Rectangles are sewed at right angles to each other. The garment stands away from the neck.

This little quexquemitl ("kesh" for short) dates back to about the fifteenth century. It is associated with abundance and fertility, and worn predominantly by women, more for ornamentation than need. It looks just like a little baby poncho. The ones I have are bright, hand-woven, coarse wool with fringed ends. Sometimes tassels are added at the points, for it is worn so there is a triangle in front and back.

BASIC PONCHO

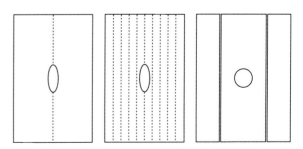

LEFT: Basic poncho. With head opening cut on straight of grain, the corners will drape to sides of body. RIGHT: Same poncho, with head opening cut on diagonal. Corners will now form triangles in front and back and over arms.

LEFT: Two strips of fabric sewn together with opening for head. CENTER: Narrow strips sewed together. RIGHT: Three strips joined; this poncho, from Guatemala, totals 36" wide, 28" long.

PONCHO

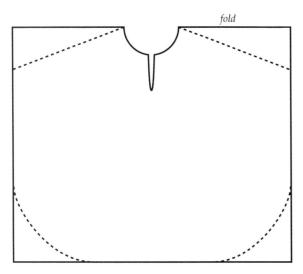

fold

A basic poncho shape. Fabric is folded horizontally, and neck opening cut out and finished. Garment may also be seamed on dotted lines which eliminates excess fabric at shoulders. This seam will change the drape. Bottom edges may be rounded.

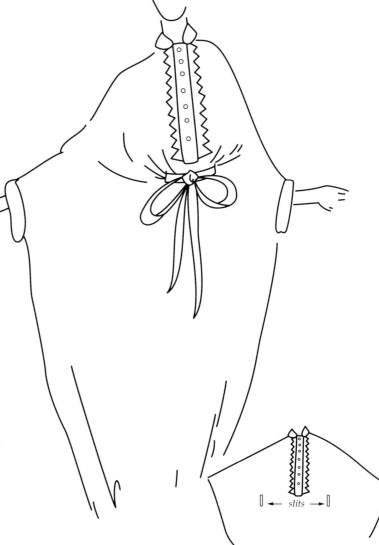

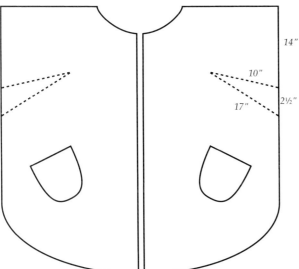

14"
10"
17" 2½"

This coat/poncho was made from a length of wool flannel 96" long and 54" wide, folded in half crosswise. The dotted lines are not for a dart; they are stitching lines through both layers, 14" down from shoulder fold, to form a sleeve-like opening. Add a collar or scarf. Overlap fronts and button at neck. Add patch pockets.

← *slits* →

A basic poncho converted to evening outfit. It is lengthened to ankles, with embellished and buttoned neck opening. There are buttonhole-like slits on each side above the waistline; a sash or belt worn under the poncho comes through the slits and fastens in front. Slits may be added to back also.

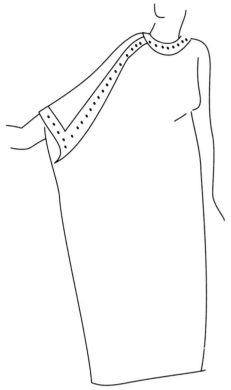

A one-shouldered evening poncho fashioned after a Senegalese "boubou." Shoulder seam is brought forward and outlined in rhinestones or beads or embroidery.

PONCHO

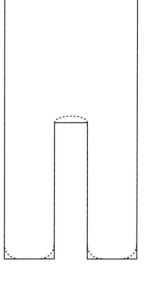

A basic poncho shape with front opening. Corners and neck may be rounded. Instead of space between two fronts, fabric may be split and faced with velvet ribbon. This is also called a U-shaped or horseshoe shaped poncho.

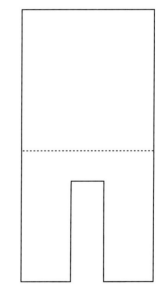

In this poncho, note how front opening is cut *below* the shoulder line. This garment will drape differently with back longer than front.

A long, narrow poncho-stole. Easy to make in unlined wool jersey; also effective in a heavy slipper satin, lined. The satin is heavy enough to form a little standing collar to frame the face.

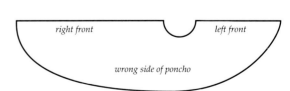

right front   *left front*

wrong side of poncho

A long "half-circle" or oval of fabric creates a different type of poncho, with neck off-center. The long side is worn on the right, and it is thrown over the left shoulder for a touch of drama.

HALF-CIRCLE GARMENTS

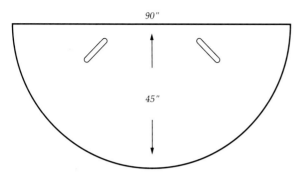

A Portuguese cape from a half circle with slits for arms.

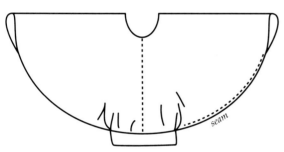

A full circle of fabric used as a blouse or jacket, found in several cultures. The measurement of the diameter is the distance from wrist to wrist with arms outstretched. The circle is folded in half. Leave a six- or seven-inch opening on each side for arms, and seam the outer edges of the circle together below the sleeve opening to within twelve inches of the center front. Gather the sections on both sides of center front and stitch to a waistband. When worn as a blouse, the center front is not cut. When worn as a jacket, the center is opened and finished. The sleeve openings are finished with a rolled or small turned hem; they may also be gathered into a cuff if wider opening is left.

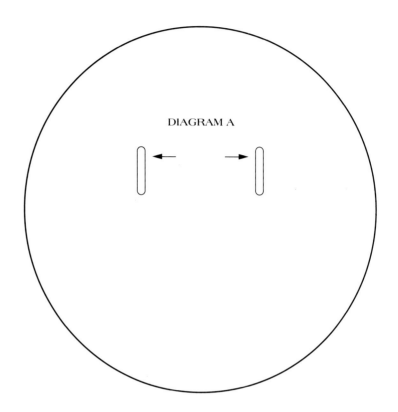

DIAGRAM A

Diagram A. Circle used as a cape, with slits for arms. When worn, top part of circle folds back, as in Diagram B.

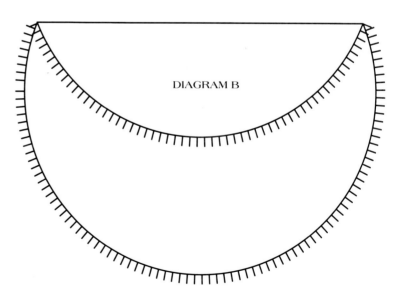

DIAGRAM B

HALF-CIRCLE SKIRT

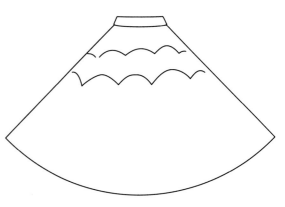

Front view of half-circle skirt with scallop design. Design might be appliqued band or applique and embroidery.

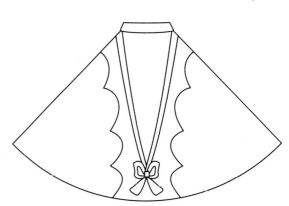

Back view of half-circle skirt. Velvet or satin ribbon stitched to a V in back and finished with bow. Zipper concealed on one edge of ribbon at waistline.

ABOVE: Full circle for skirt or cape.
BELOW: Half circle for skirt or cape.

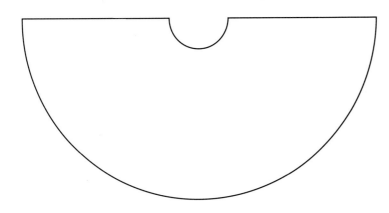

TABARDS

Tabard or tunic fastened at sides with strip.

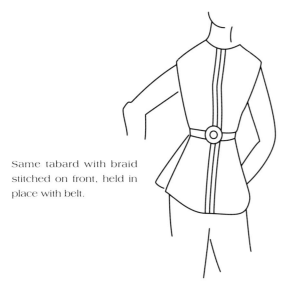

Same tabard with braid stitched on front, held in place with belt.

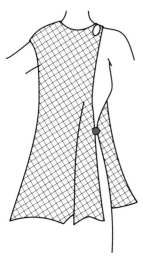

One-shoulder tabard. This tabard or tunic is made from two rectangles, perhaps 12 or 14" wide, and hangs about 7" below the waist. It slips over the head and can be fastened at the sides. It can also be belted, and the front trimmed with braid, ribbon or embroidery. It can be lined or not.

TABARDS OR TUNICS

Tabards or tunics are usually longer than waist length, thus made of rectangles rather than squares. You can easily make one from two basic rectangles fastened at the shoulder points and again at the sides near the waistline. You can also shape the neckline rather than leave it straight across; you can belt it or not, and it can be any length. Elaine Zinn's tabard, shown in Chapter 8, *Accessories*, is ankle-length and could be worn over pants as well as a skirt.

CAFTANS

The caftan originally came from Persia, but there are variations of it in Africa, Mexico and America, to name a few. It is a straight paneled dress, again composed of rectangles, with square-cut sleeves and a side panel. It can be adapted to anything from a beach cover-up to an evening or at-home dress.

A cloth rectangle is the base for the cape coat shown on page 23, as well as the basic shape of the Japanese kimono. Once you discover the ease and excitement of working with ethnic shapes, you'll wonder how you ever got along without them.

With a little time and patience, it wouldn't be difficult for you to figure out your own pattern for some of these ethnic styled garments, but I'll make life a little easier for you. I've worked with these styles for several years and developed diagrams and measurements which have turned out to be more than satisfactory. My students create exciting and colorful garments by using these diagrams, then going on into color and design. In this book, I'm including several of the patterns I've developed, along with instructions for assembly, so if you follow these pages you can have some wonderful wearables of your own before you know it. I've also included an in-seam pocket pattern for you; traditionally, many of these garments have no pockets; the sleeves of the Japanese kimonos serve as pockets, for instance, but I'm so thoroughly American I need to go a step further. You could add patch pockets if you like, or but-

DIAGRAM A

Diagram A: Diagram for medium size: This is a loose fitting jacket. *Diagram B:* Body of garment. *Diagram C:* Neckband. Cut 5" wide for 2" finished band. *Diagram D:* Sleeves. Cut 2 of base fabric, 2 of outside and 2 of lining. *Diagram E:* How to fold sleeve. Shown is right sleeve; reverse for left. Diagram F: Neckline detail. Dotted line is staystitching through garment, base or filler, and lining. Clip to corners.

DIAGRAM C

30"

DIAGRAM B

DIAGRAM D

14"

7"

fold

7"

seam

14"

fold

28"

DIAGRAM E

length 80" = full length
length 60" = hip length

neckband to fit front opening

shoulder

6"

7"

7"

14"

14"

14"

DIAGRAM F

5"

12"

12"

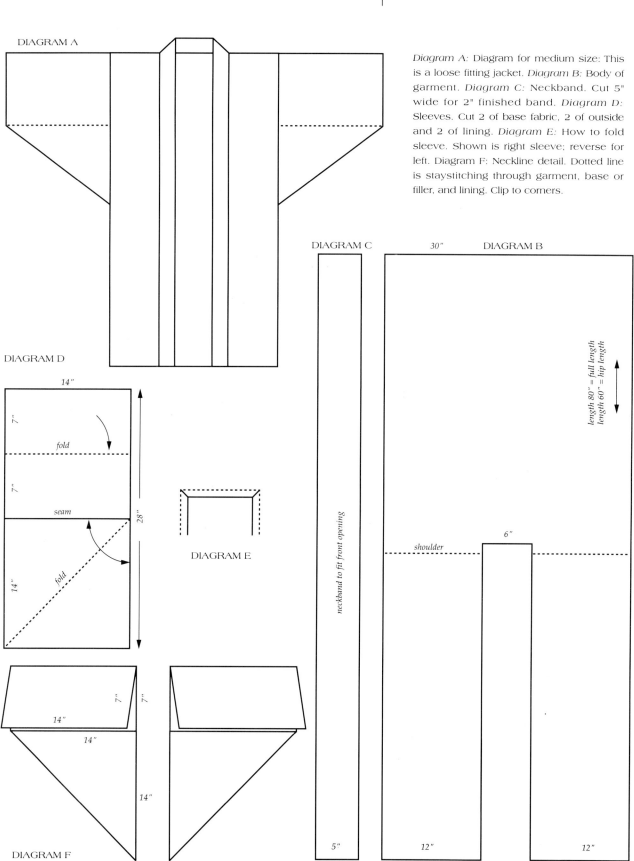

SLEEVES

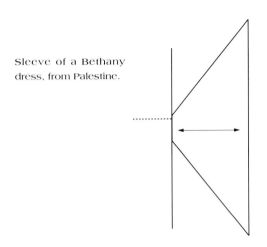

Sleeve of a Bethany dress, from Palestine.

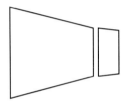

Sleeve from a deerskin jacket of NAHAN tribe, Canada.

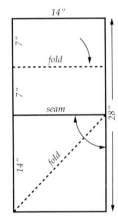

Variation of the folded sleeve, this one from a burnoose, N. Africa.

KIMONOS

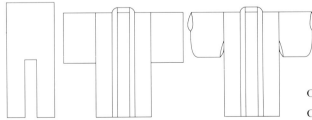

LEFT: Basic cutting shape of the Japanese kimono. CENTER: Hapi coat version, with squared-off open sleeves. RIGHT: Haori coat with a traditional sleeve. All garments have similar neckbands, either full-length or shortened.

- Develop your design for body of coat and sleeves and sew to foundation. Work on sleeves simultaneously, folding them in proper sequence so you will end up with a right and left sleeve.
- Cut out lining same as coat.
- Stitch coat and lining side seams separately below armscye (sleeve opening). Press seams open. Fit lining into coat, wrong sides together, matching raw edges, and pin.
- Staystitch neck edge through coat and lining. Clip to corners.
- Stitch neckband to coat through coat and lining, right sides together. Turn neckband toward lining side and hand finish.
- Bind hem edge of coat, through coat and lining together.
- Stitch sleeve and sleeve lining seams separately, press open. This seam is shown as the dotted line across sleeves in Diagram A.
- Fit lining inside sleeve, wrong sides together. Bind lower edge or add cuff or extension. Pin armscye edges together.
- Stitch sleeve to coat, holding back coat lining in this area; hand finish coat lining over sleeve seam.

Although this coat is patterned after the ones worn in northern Japanese islands, it is similar to the 19th century coat worn by men of the Horuriku region of Japan, and the same folded sleeve is used in garments of North Africa.

I also adapted this coat/jacket for Japanese 16th century patchwork, the technique for which is included in the book section on piecing.

JAPANESE KIMONO

The Japanese kimono is one of our greatest gifts from the Orient. In its home country, it is bound by centuries of tradition and design, seasons and station in life, but here in America we embrace its simple T-shape and use it in many ways, adapting it to our various lifestyles. It can be casual and sporty in cotton, elegant in silk or satin. We don't use the Japanese obi, but we may add a belt or change the sleeves or neckline, still maintaining the simple and functional outline.

In Japan, the sleeves in a kimono for formal wear are different for a man and woman. A man's sleeve is sharp edged, the woman's rounded at the bottom. Kimono fabric is loomed 14" wide, a most economical width, and the strips seamed together to create the garment. Since so many of the ethnic shapes are similar, surface design and pattern emerge from all of them with primary importance.

THE BOG COAT JACKET

This is everybody's favorite, and since I started teaching Bog Coat classes several years ago, the classes have been full and there is always a waiting list. This coat, as with the other ethnic garments, can be made for any climate, any occasion and any person, and that's a combination hard to beat.

This garment is pre-historic, reputedly the oldest in clothing history. Where the name "bog" came from, no one quite knows, but it has stuck, and we're stuck with it. Its history is sketchy. Originally unearthed in Denmark in about 1000 BC (early Bronze Age), it has resurfaced intermittently in different cultures and times. Here in America, it fits beautifully into contemporary wardrobes. Margot Carter Blair reports that it appeared in Egypt about 600 AD, probably influenced by the Persians who wore the cut as late as the 19th century – but made of felt. Margot also reports that similar garments are found in India, worn by the women of Rajpulana.

The original of the Danish garment, or what's left of it, is in the National Museum of Copenhagen, but a photo of it, worn and frayed, is shown in the Time/Life *Art of Sewing* series in the *Classic Techniques* volume. The same photo appears in Boucher's *Twenty Thousand Years of Fashion*. Max Tilke, in his *Costume Patterns and Designs*, shows the Bog Coat as a garment from Persia, the original Iranian garment, with the same horizontal cut. It also appears in Dorothy K. Burnham's wonderful little book, *Cut My Cote*, a publication of the Royal Ontario Museum of Toronto. Ms. Burnham adds an interesting historical note in attributing the cut to early skin garments; she suggests that a large animal skin would fold around the body with no side seams. (And so

KIMONO SLEEVES

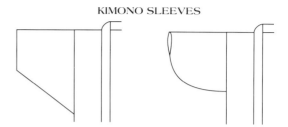

LEFT: Man's sleeve, Japan. RIGHT: Woman's sleeve, Japan.

John Mangiapane's bog coat. Cotton, with Oriental designs.

"The Scots Stop Here," a bog coat of wool plaid and gold lame. Designed and made by the author.

Bog Raincoat by Susan Jones. This coat may be worn plain, or with the carp-design body ornament shown in Chapter 8 on page 149. The outfit is called, fittingly enough, "Stop Carping About the Weather".

COLLAR

Mandarin-type collar for garments. Length may be adjusted to fit neck edge. See page 161 for full-size pattern. A bias fold of fabric is a good substitute for a collar; use a layer of interfacing inside the folds.

too, will a large piece of fabric!) She also shows the garment in miniature, as used for infants' clothes in the 18th and 19th centuries.

In the early 1970's, I saw the Balenciaga exhibit at the Metropolitan Museum of Art in New York City – and guess what! Balenciaga's much publicized one-seam coat, shown on a mannequin, was nothing more than the Bog Coat! He was indeed the Master of Couture in cut, design, exquisite workmanship and finishing. His adoption of the Bog Coat was a manifestation of his vision. In that exhibit, the muslin pattern was also shown on a mannequin, and the paper pattern pinned on the wall behind them. Balenciaga had lengthened the coat to street length; he added pockets and a collar and extended the front for a lapped closing. He also added a couple of darts for fitting in the shoulder and hips, but it was the same coat, and he made several versions of it in perfectly matched plaid wool.

The major fascination in this garment is the economy of fabric and the fact that it has one seam – this seems unbelievable to those of us who sew. The coat can be lined or not; made of wool, or a small blanket; use any wonderful fabric you have in your stash and have hesitated to cut, for the cut is minimal. Of course you can design your own outer shell; piece or applique it, quilt it, or use that wallhanging or quilt you never finished.

On page 29 you'll find the working diagrams for the Bog Coat/Jacket; if you're puzzled by the diagram, trace it, cut it out, then fold and cut as directions indicate, and voila! There it is. Margot Carter Blair, in her series on ethnic clothing, has especially good instructions and diagrams for the seamed version, and she has graciously permitted me to include them on page 30.

BOG COAT/JACKET INSTRUCTIONS

(Lined or Unlined Coat with Bound Edges)

- Measure bust and hips; use largest measurement and add 6" for ease. This is the width of your working fabric AB and CD, on cross grain of fabric. If your required measurement is wider than 45" and you are using whole-cloth fabric, add to get required width, or turn fabric and use the length-wise grain for AB.

- To determine length of coat, have someone measure you in back from mid-shoulder to finished length. Add 12" to this; this measurement is AC and BD.

- Mark mid-point between A and B; this is center front.

- Mark 12" down on AC and BD and pin or threadbaste this horizontal line; it is the shoulder fold dotted line in the diagram. (Note: if you want a narrower sleeve, try 10" or 11" instead of 12".)

- Measure the same distance down from the shoulder fold line, and mark a line parallel to the shoulder fold ¼ of the width. This is the sleeve cut. DO NOT CUT.

- To mark center front and neck opening, draw a per-pendicular line from center front mark on AB to 1" past the shoulder fold line. This is the back neck mark. Now, from the intersection of the center front and shoulder fold line, mark 3" on each side of the shoulder fold line, and 3" down on center front line. Join these four marks for the neck opening. Remember, the back neck is 1" past the shoulder fold line.

- Cut lining. Place lining against outside shell, wrong sides together, matching outside edges and pinning securely. Staystitch through both thicknesses ¼" on either side of center front line and on neck opening line. Cut between the lines of stitching and ¼" inside the neck opening. Clip curves.

- Staystitch ¼" on either side of sleeve cut, through all thicknesses; round-or square-off end of stitching. Cut between stitched lines. If you want to add a sleeve extension, now is the time to do it. Bind sleeve cuts. Pin garment together and try it on to see if neck opening is O.K. If so, add collar if desired; other-wise, bind center front opening and neck edge.

- Finish binding all outside edges. Turn garment over so that wrong side or lining side is facing you. Fold top down along shoulder fold line to form sleeves. Below sleeve cut, fold AC and BD toward center. The coat is now T-shaped and you are ready to join the one-seam (sleeve-bodice) together.

- These edges butt together; there is no provision for

BOG COAT/JACKET

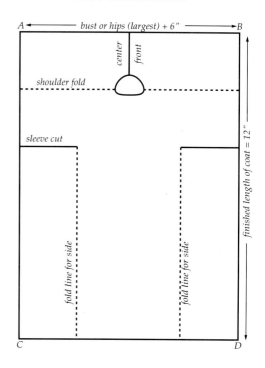

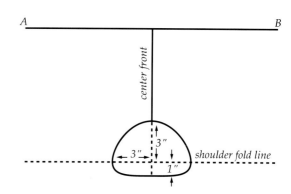

Enlargement of center front and neck opening for Bog Coat.

Margot Carter Blair's Bog Coat with Lining and Seamed Edges

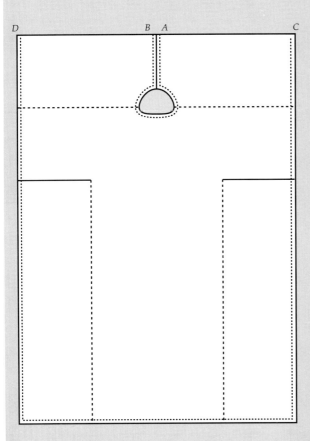

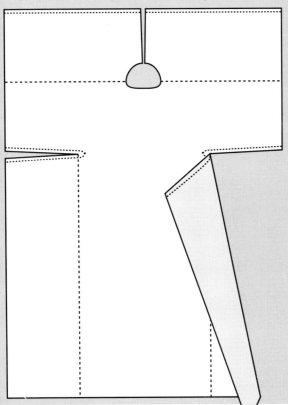

LEFT TOP: Construction of Bog Coat with lining: neck and outside seams. Pin garment fabric and lining fabric together, right sides facing. Stitch around center front and neck opening through both layers, then stitch around outside from AC to CD to DB. The two top edges on either side of front opening will be open. Trim seams and turn through a top opening. Press.

LEFT BOTTOM: Sleeve seams. Staystitch the sleeve marking on both sides of as yet uncut slit, forming long narrow U-shape line. Cut on the sleeve marking, between the two lines of stay-stitching, clipping almost to stitching line at the turn.

Baste top front raw edges together.

BELOW: Finishing front top and sleeve seams. Make your own bias tape to finish raw edges. For single bias, cut strips 1" wide to finish at ¼": for double bias, cut strips 1½" wide, fold in half lengthwise and press, raw edges together. Match raw edges of binding to raw edges of fronts and sleeve openings and stitch, using ¼" seams. Finish by hand. If you want ties in front to fasten coat, add 10" to front bindings or add the ties later.

Use #5 perle cotton for blanket stitch over the binding, then lace seams together with faggoting stitch or by crocheting edges together.

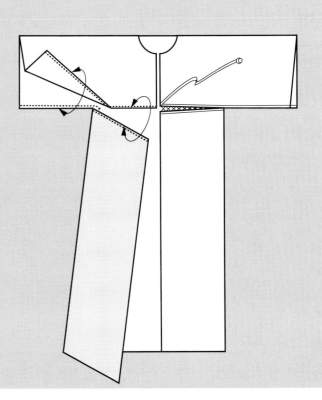

BOG COAT/JACKET VARIATIONS

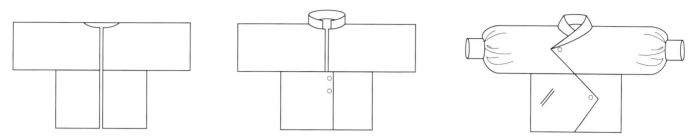

LEFT: Regular Bog Coat with sleeve cut ¼ of fabric width. Fronts meet. May be fastened with frogs or ties. CENTER: Bog Coat with sleeve cut longer than ¼ of width. Lower front overlaps. Mandarin collar added. RIGHT: Bog Coat with cuff extensions added. Sleeve may also be extended without gathers. Both top and lower fronts have extensions for closing. Slot pocket on one side.

seam allowance. You may blind-stitch this seam together or machine stitch with zigzag or decorative stitch. You can use blanket stitch to cover bindings, then lace perle cotton through stitches; another way is to use insertion or faggoting stitch, a cretan or her-ringbone stitch, or join edges with single crochet. Lastly, you can close this seam with loops and but-tons.

In the instructions I gave you, the sleeve cut is designated at ¼ of the width. This insures the fronts meet at the center. If the sleeve cut is longer than ¼, there will be a lap-over as shown in center diagram above. The diagram, above right, shows further varia-tions; extensions added to sleeves and both top and bottom fronts for an asymmetrical closing. There is also a slot pocket on one side.

The Bog Coat/Jacket makes up quickly in a pre-quilted fabric, whether it's yours or store-bought. It can also be unlined, perhaps of Mexican or Guatemalan cotton, hand-woven or other wool, or chiffon, silk crepe or silk noil. It's truly a coat for all seasons.

THE COCOON COAT

Doesn't the idea of a cocoon coat sound cozy? It is. It is a coat/jacket which wraps around the body, hugging it, and it does resemble a cocoon a little bit. Like so many others, this garment is made from a rectangle, and the diagram is a no-pattern pattern.

The diagram/pattern on page 32 is for a cocoon coat with pleated fullness in the back and at front shoulders, and it takes about three yards of fabric. If

COCOON COAT

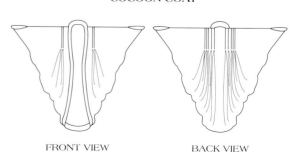

FRONT VIEW   BACK VIEW

WORKING DIAGRAM FOR COCOON COAT

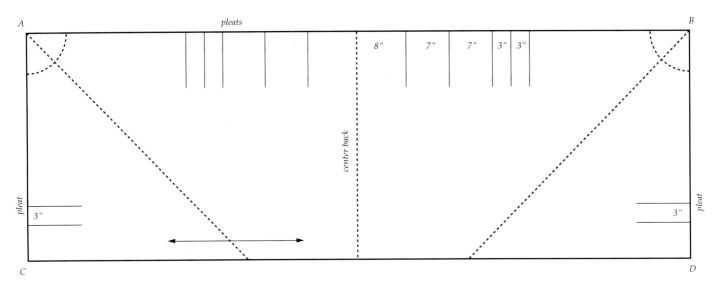

COCOON COAT INSTRUCTIONS

AB and CD are about 3 yards in length. Width, AC and BD, is your choice, and may be width of fabric (36", 45").

Mark center back on length AB. On each side, form 8" pleat to make a box pleat; on either side of box pleat, add two 7" pleats and two 3" pleats. Stitch these down 6 or 7".

On AC and BD, make two 3" pleats; stitch down.

Now fold AC on diagonal line so that edges are at right angles to each other. Do the same with BD. Seam AC along AB line, leaving 10" opening at end of fabric for sleeve. Repeat for other side. Hem sleeve opening. Finish outside edges with binding or neck band up to 2" wide.

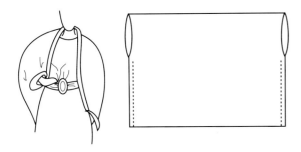

Variation of the cocoon coat, using crosswise fold of fabric. The lower edges, bound all around, become the front opening.

you have less fabric, or want a coat without pleats, you can still follow the diagram. Lay the fabric out on a flat surface in front of you, then fold up each end at right angles to the top selvage, and seam these edges together, leaving a 9" or 10" opening at the end for your hands. Stitch a 2" band entirely around the outer edges to finish it, or use a narrow binding.

A variation of the cocoon coat is to fold the fabric crosswise as shown in the diagram. Seam the sides together, leaving an opening at the fold for your arms to go through. Bind the raw edges of the opening; this becomes the outer edge which goes around the neck and waist, as in the drawing of the completed jacket.

THE OTHELLO COAT

This is another one of those ravishing rectangles. It doesn't pre-date history, but it certainly fits into today's life styles – as a beach cover-up or a great casual jacket to wear with jeans, or as a dramatic wrap for evening. Again, it works as well in wool as it does in cotton. It is a rectangle with two seams, and it can be made vertically or horizontally.

I first saw this coat several years ago at an exhibit in New York City which featured costumes for stage productions. An assistant curator made it possible for me to get a good close look at it, but at the time the garment had no name. Some years later, I ran across it again, this time in the book *Exotic Needlework* by Dona Z. Meilach and Dee Menagh; the two authors credited Frances Bardacke with the name "Othello Coat," for the coat was originally made and worn in a Shakespearean play. Since that time I have played around with it, as I like to do with many of these intriguing pieces, and eventually worked up a couple of diagrams to use as a guide or pattern. Margot Carter Blair also includes a diagram for this coat in her ethnic clothing portfolio. It looks shapeless and squared off to the un-seasoned eye and needs the human body to give it motion and life.

Two measurements are required. With your arms outstretched, have someone measure you across the back from wrist to wrist. Double this; you will probably need 2½ to 3 yards. The longest seam, (second seam) is the wrist-to-wrist one and falls across the back shoulders when the coat is worn.

Diagram 1 shows you how simple the construction is. The two crosswise grain ends are put together and seamed from A to B. The length of this seam is a matter of preference, and it will affect the drape of the coat. I suggest you pin the two seams together and try the coat on before you do any sewing. This seam, the first seam to be sewed, should be no longer than half the width of the fabric and might look better if it were much less – this is for you to decide. Once you have stitched this seam, (A to B), match it to the mid-point of the fabric, shown as B in the diagram. Now stitch the second seam, (C to D), leaving a 9" or 10" opening at each end for your hands. Now try the coat on; if you have used the full width of the fabric, 45", it will be a full-length coat. If you want to shorten it, simply measure up from the bottom and cut off a strip. Bind or hem the raw edges.

This coat may be lined or not.

If you prefer a coat a little less voluminous, use a measurement of elbow to elbow with arms outstretched instead of wrist-to-wrist. You can also stitch a tube of fabric to the arm opening to make sleeves.

Diagram 2 shows a variation of this coat. The main difference is the sleeve or arm opening. In the

"Othello" coat by Margot Carter Blair. Pieced cotton; made for Fairfield-Concord Fashion Show. Photo: Brad Stanton.

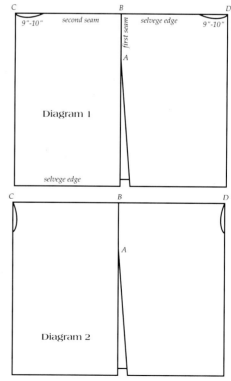

The seams are the same, but this time the sleeve opening is cut down into the fabric and finished with a narrow hem. The placement of the sleeve or arm opening affects the drape as coat is worn.

OTHELLO COAT

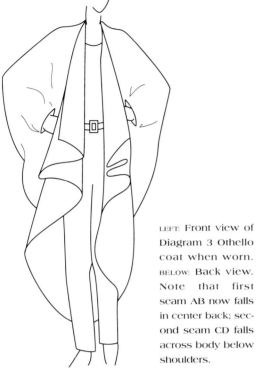

LEFT: Front view of Diagram 3 Othello coat when worn. BELOW: Back view. Note that first seam AB now falls in center back; second seam CD falls across body below shoulders.

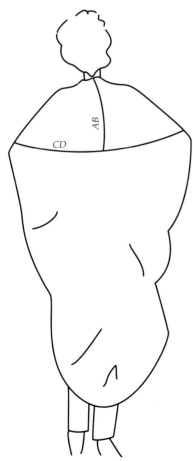

first coat, the opening is at the top along the selvage edge. The second coat shows the sleeve opening cut into the fold of fabric at the coat sides; these raw edges will have to be bound or otherwise finished. The location of the arm openings makes a difference in the way the coat drapes.

The coat on the figure at left is Diagram 3. In this version, the first seam is stitched for half the width of the fabric; this makes the coat much longer in back.

INSTRUCTIONS FOR A LINED GARMENT

Cut lining and shell identical. Stitch the first seam in each, press open and clip at bottom edge. Slip lining inside the shell, right sides facing. Starting at lower edge of first seam, stitch down toward hem through shell and lining, matching raw edges. Pivot at hem edge; stitch around hem edge and pivot again; stitch other side of front opening up to starting point at lower edge of first seam. Trim seam allowance if necessary, cut excess fabric from corners, turn and press.

Match top of first seam to mid-point on CD. Right sides together, stitch front to back, holding back the back lining. Layer or trim seam. Fold under raw edge of held-back lining and hand finish over seam. This join could be embellished with embroidery or covered with braid or ribbon. Bind arm opening or tuck raw edges in against each other and blind-stitch by hand.

A few years ago I met a young designer in Ontario and he suggested still another version of the Othello coat. He omitted the first seam and instead, left a 5" space where the ends of the fabric length met the selvage edge, as in Diagram 5. He also suggested shortening the coat to jacket length and the finished version was about 27" or 28" long. He bordered all the outside edges with ornamental braid and used tassels for decoration.

Although we call this the "Othello Coat," the garment is very similar to the aba or abaya, a garment worn in the Middle East.

Like the cocoon coat, you may change the Othello coat by using the fabric horizontally instead of vertically for a different look and drape. In Diagram 6 both the first and second seams are eliminated and

OTHELLO COAT

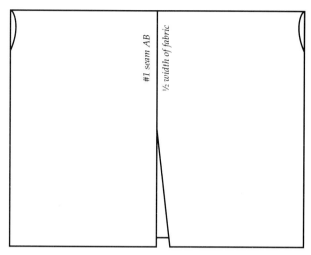

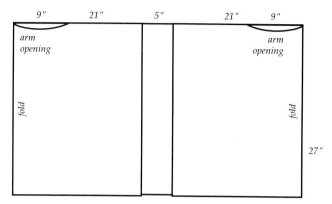

Diagram 3

In this version, the sleeve openings are those of Diagram 2. However, the first seam, AB, is stitched one-half the width of fabric instead of the shorter version in Diagram 1. This longer seam causes the coat to drape entirely differently; it is perhaps more dramatic, dipping in back.

Diagram 5

In this version, the ends of the length of fabric are folded toward the center, leaving a 5" space. Seam fabric front to back along top edge, leaving arm openings free. Finish all raw edges.

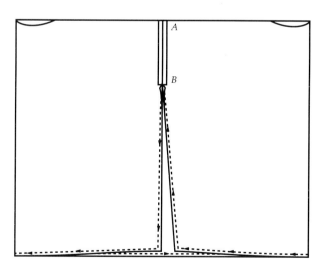

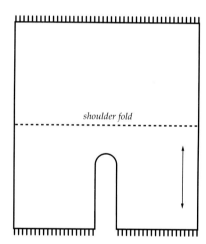

Diagram 4

If you wish to line the Othello coat, cut shell and lining and stitch No. 1 seam in both. Press seams open and clip at end of stitching so they will lie flat.

Put the two fabrics together, right sides facing each other and seams matching. Pin. Now stitch from below end of No. 1 seam (AB) to hem corner; pivot; stitch around hem to other corner; pivot again; stitch back up front to seam. Trim seam, turn and press.

Line up No. 2 seam, raw edges matching. Hold back the back lining section, stitch through other three thicknesses; trim seam; turn under raw edge of back lining fabric and hand finish over seam.

Diagram 6

ABOVE: The Othello coat cut vertically instead of horizontally. Only side seams need to be stitched, but neck opening should be hemmed or faced. Lower edges of garment may be hemmed, faced or fringed.

BELOW: Fold fabric in half as diagram shows. Stitch side seams from below sleeve opening to bottom. Cuffs or sleeve extensions may also be added.

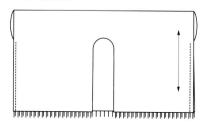

Long vest by Ardis James, using an Yvonne Porcella pattern. A strip of Afghani patchwork decorates a front panel.

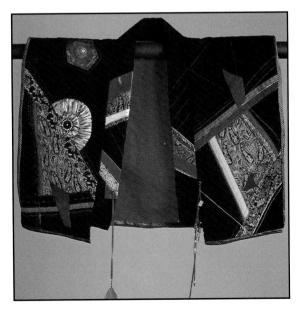

Short version of "terrific tunic vest," with neck band. By Beryl Maddelena.

instead, there are side seams to be stitched. You can see from the diagram the neck opening is cut below the shoulder line to give drape to the back. Staystitch the front opening before you cut, then bind the edges or face them with velvet ribbon. If you leave the side seams open instead of stitching them, you have a version of the poncho instead of the Othello Coat. That's the name of the game.

VESTS

Vest patterns are almost a dime a dozen; all the pattern companies print at least one or two versions and there are a number of patterns self-published which are sold in quilt shops or at conferences. Some vests are long, some are short; some are cut in high and some have extended shoulders. Some are to be worn open, some are closed with a button or frog and others are double-breasted, and all of this means, of course, that any and all styles are at your disposal.

The vest which is really unique, however, is the one I want to tell you about, and it is another which I also teach in workshops as the Great Garment Tunic Vest or Crazy Collage Tunic Vest – it is both. My friend Beryl discovered it, an old beat-up leather vest someone had given her. She almost threw it away then decided to try it on and that did it. She couldn't wait to tell me about it and show it to me, and both of us worked out patterns for it. Mine has been diagrammed for use in workshops and for this book; the color photos will give you an idea of some of the possibilities, and the diagram on page 37 will get you started making one of your own. The measurements given here are for a medium size, so you will need to scale it down if you are smaller and add to it if you are larger. If you need to make it bigger, increase the side panel rather than the body of the tunic vest. You can shorten it to waist length and add a neck band, as Beryl did in the photo at left, or you can make it as is.

GENERAL INSTRUCTIONS FOR TUNIC VEST

Working on a foundation or base fabric, complete the design for the outside, piecing, applique, quilting, collage, etc. Cut the lining the same as the outside. The front opening may be seamed instead of bound.

To do this, place lining against outside layer, right sides together, with raw edges matched and pinned. Remember the back neck extends 1" past the shoulder line to insure a better fit. Stitch up one front, around neck and down the other side, using ½" seam allowance. Trim seam, clip neck curves, turn lining to inside and press. Run a line of top stitching ¼" from the seam all the way around.

If you are binding all edges, skip the paragraph above. Fit lining to outer shell, wrong sides together, matching raw edges; then add binding.

Next, seam or bind across the top edge of the side panel through the outer shell and lining; then pin the sides of the panel to the sides of the tunic, starting at bottom. Bind through all thicknesses; starting at the bottom, go over the shoulder and down the other side to the bottom hem edge. Bind the bottom hem edge, catching all raw edges.

For a change of pace, you can use a 2" neckband instead of a seamed or bound finish.

This tunic is designed to be worn closed. Use two big fancy buttons, a frog, ties with tassel and beads or a buckle as the photos show.

Back view of zebra "terrific tunic vest" by the author, shown on page 11.

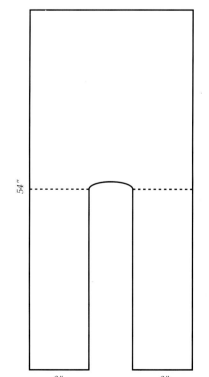

**GREAT GARMENT
TUNIC VEST**

2½"

15"

3½"

An essential piece to add to your wardrobe; wonderful to wear, easy to make. You can lengthen it, shorten it, add shoulder flanges, add a collar or a neckband. Use any fabrics – silk, cotton, linen, wool, velvet, corduroy, decorator fabrics, solids, plaids or stripes. Use any techniques – piecing, applique, collage, quilting, embellishments; let your imagination take over.

54"

8"   8"

ABOVE: Front view of "terrific tunic vest" by Beryl Maddelena; collection of the author. BELOW: Back view of vest.

A PATTERN WRAP-UP: THE BOTTOM LINE

Once you've discovered how easy and how satisfying it is to make your special garments, your own wonderful wearables, you won't ever want to stop. The time you spend on designing and sewing will pay you enormous dividends and a burst of creativity is like a shot in the arm. The pattern/diagrams I've given you in this book may not fill all your needs, but they will certainly help. Buy your basics and your classics, then fill in with jackets and other garments. I think jackets are probably the most important item in anyone's wardrobe and even in hot weather a lightweight jacket or wrap completes your outfit. A jacket – or vest for that matter – adds to a dress, to skirts and pants, and the colors and fabrics you've used in it are there for all to see.

Choose patterns with good cut and style, and you can use them over and over again. As for basics in patterns, you should have a jacket or coat pattern with raglan sleeve, one with a set-in sleeve, one with a dropped-shoulder sleeve and one with a square-cut sleeve – and you could also add a dolman sleeve. With these to fall back on, you would be ready for anything.

All of the wearables we've talked about require only simple sewing and even if you haven't had a lot of experience, you won't have any trouble. The garments are put together with straight seams, and even the finishing techniques aren't complicated.

I hope you have a sewing space of your own, but even if you don't, there are ways to make-do. A dining room table can serve double duty for eating and cutting. You can also make a work and cutting top with very little money and trouble. Use a 4' x 8' sheet of plywood, pad it lightly and cover it with muslin. It can fit over a much smaller table or even over sawhorses and give you the cutting area you need. When you aren't using it, store it by standing it against the wall and using it for pin-up work.

You know how important it is to have good sewing supplies, too – pins, needles, threads, marking and measuring tools and good scissors. Your cutting shears should be sharp – well, all your scissors should be sharp and they should cut cleanly to the point. Applique or "pelican" scissors are good to have for extras, for the wide blade protects you from cutting into your fabric when that is the last thing you want to do! Rotary cutters and their self-healing mats are important sewing supplies: then of course you need a thimble, some beeswax, a seam ripper and some masking and transparent tape. There are assorted see-through rulers available and I still like to use a tape measure for many things. As for marking tools, I don't like the water-soluble pens and I don't encourage my students to use them. I wouldn't want to have to get my work wet to remove the marks, and I think there are other things more satisfactory. I use the new chalk markers and like them; the marks are quite visible, and although they don't last very long, they last long enough for me to complete my stitching or quilting and I can easily brush any residue off. I also use soap slivers and perhaps a silver or white pencil to mark dark fabrics. Just be sure *anything* you use can be removed.

Take good care of your sewing machine, for it's one of your best friends. Keep it oiled and lint free, and have extra needles and bobbins on hand. Sometimes we forget how important sewing machines are; they're almost indispensible to our lives. The upholstery and slip covers of our furniture, the curtains and draperies for our windows, our kitchen, bed and bath linens are all sewed by machine, so we need to give these marvelous inventions the respect they deserve. In the past few years, machines have become computerized and they are indeed marvels. Although I have a couple of "old-fashioned machines," I do have a computerized machine, too, and I'm fascinated with it. Mine does almost everything but talk and I do not want it to start that – ever; no whining and complaining from the sewing room!

Many of you may have sergers, and, especially if you do a lot of sewing, they can save a great deal of time for you; children's clothes and home sewing both benefit. Good pressing is just as important as good sewing, but I'm sure you know that. One of the first rules in sewing I ever learned was "Don't sew over an unpressed seam." It's a good rule and it can mean the difference between a homemade look and

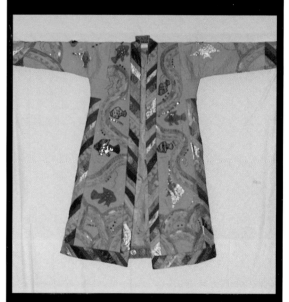

"Fishyssoise" by Ann Boyce.

Barbara State's Turkish coat, front view.

Continued on pages 40-41

EAST MEETS WEST

"Amish Coat" back view, by Kim Masopust.
Model: Mary Mashuta.

"Seattle Spring" by Laura Munson Reinstatler.
©1986 Laura Munson Reinstatler.

a professional look. Along with your iron (or irons) and board, you should have a press mitt and a tailor's ham to help you press special areas.

Most of the seams you sew will be straight ones for construction and if your garment is lined, they will be concealed. There is no standard seam allowance; some commercial patterns use ⅝", some use ½" and some use ¼". Check this out before you start sewing and follow the printed instructions included in the pattern. These are carefully written and they are pretty good road maps.

Seams need to be finished in unlined garments and there are several ways of doing this. You can flat-fell them (see page 43), or turn under the raw edge of each seam and topstitch. You can cover the seams with braid or ribbon (a strap seam), but the stitching will show on the right side unless you sew the seams to the outside.

One of the most elegant and practical seam and hem finishes is the Hong Kong finish, and I'd like to tell you how to do that. For every raw edge to be covered or enclosed, cut a bias strip 1½" wide. Be sure it is true bias, otherwise it will twist and ripple and you'll never get it to lie flat. The 1½" width may be a little wide for some fabrics, but it will be fine for most, especially if you have a layer of base fabric or a layer of thin batting to cover too. Right sides together, lay one edge of the bias strip against the garment, raw edges matching, and stitch a ½" seam. Trim seam to ⅛" or ¼", depending on the thickness of the fabric. Now press the bias strip up and over the raw edge to be enclosed; then, working from the right side, stitch in the ditch for the final step. Trim the bias close to the stitching line. Bias does not ravel, so it needs no further attention.

When lining a garment, seam the edges, bind them, or use a combination of both. Binding is probably the easiest, and I like to use a French or double bias in matching or contrasting fabric. This bias is stronger than a single one, and easier to handle since you don't have to turn under any raw edges when hand stitching the bias to the inside. For a ½" finished binding, cut a true bias strip 3" wide, fold in half lengthwise and press lightly. This allows for two ½" seam allowances, a double ½" binding for the outside and a double ½" for the inside. Match the raw edges of the bias strip to the raw edge of garment, right sides together and stitch. Trim seam slightly. Press bias up and over seam allowances, and hand finish through folded edge to the stitching line.

If you are seaming at ¼" and want a ¼" bias binding for finishing, cut your true bias strip 1½" wide, fold in the middle lengthwise and press lightly; then follow directions as listed above.

I used the Hong Kong finish on the quilted lining panels of the coat in my "There's a Hot Time in the Old Town Tonight" outfit. When each of the panel edges was encased with the bias, I butted them together and zigzagged them closed with metallic thread. It was functional, kept the seams flat and also added an ornamental touch. Seams do not always need to be discreet; you can draw attention to them in a decorative way and add to the overall design.

Piping or cording will add a crisp, professional look, white faggoting or insertion stitches give a lacy, openwork appearance. Faggoting is easy. First, bind the seams then cover with a blanket stitch in perle cotton. Use the blanket stitches as a base for the insertion stitches, and try other flosses or yarns, or mini-ribbons, as well as perle cotton.

When you're sewing wonderful wearables, there is no right or wrong way to do something. There are usually several different methods to achieve the same end, so don't be afraid to explore.

EAST MEETS WEST

"Don't Shoot the Piano Player, She's Doing the Best She Can" by the author.

Back view of Elinor Peace Bailey's Turkish coat, appliqued with her unique figures and dolls.

FABRICS:
Their care and feeding

Style is always important, but fabric plays the leading role in our drama. One of the great delights in creating your own one-of-a-kind wearable is choosing and working with fabrics you love. This statement carries a lot of weight, for if you're in your right mind, you won't buy a fabric you don't like. I did once, thinking I would force myself to use it and in some way this would expand my thinking and designing; I was wrong. I never used that fabric, although I pulled it out several times in a half-hearted attempt to "do something" with it. I finally gave it away. The fabrics you choose – and the fabrics I choose – say a lot about our attitudes, our likes and dislikes. We probably all learned to sew because we had to do something creative with the fabrics we had on hand – and couldn't justify buying any more until these were used up. (Thank heaven I recovered from that guilt trip!) Our passion for fabrics seems to always be out of hand. We go on vacation and one of the first things we do is to hunt up the fabric shops while the rest of the family checks out the movies or the beaches or the pizza parlor. We'd rather spend time among the bolts and remnant bins than go to the theater or play a round of bridge. We may be somewhat defensive about it, but I think there is no cure for it; we should neither apologize nor try to explain. Each new fabric shop may carry that special color we've wanted for such a long time, and there's no harm in looking. It's nice to belong to a sewing or quilt guild too, for there you don't have to explain; everyone understands.

BASIC CONSTRUCTION TIPS

Happily, the basic seams you'll need for sewing garments are easy ones and even if you have had little sewing experience before now, you can easily conquer these seams. Seam allowances vary in patterns; most commercial patterns still use a standard ⅝" or in some cases ½". Ethnic patterns use either ½" or ¼" so it's important you check the seam allowance being used before you start to sew. It not only makes a difference in the fit, but it also makes a difference in assembling your garment.

Most seams are straight and if you've used the machine for piecing quilt tops or other such work, you've had a lot of practice with straight seams – maybe curved ones too. Be sure the machine's thread tensions are balanced, and before you do *any* machine work, do a test piece first.

If you are lining a garment, the construction seams usually will be pressed open; they do not need any special finishing since they will be concealed. If your garment is unlined – a jacket, coat or cape – you should have a neat way to finish the seams so that the raw edges will not be visible. A simple finish is to press the seam open, then turn under ⅛" on each seam edge and machine stitch it.

Flat-felling a seam is another possibility. You have to do this seam by seam, as you go along; you can't wait until you're finished then go back and do it. To flat-fell a seam, stitch the seam with the wrong sides together. Trim one seam allowance fairly close to the stitching, then turn under the raw edge of the other and top stitch it in place so that it covers the trimmed seam allowance. This is a sporty finish rather than an elegant one.

We must not forget how greatly fabrics are entwined with our lives. They supply our personal shelter, and if hunger is the foremost human instinct, surely shelter is the second. Fabric protects peasants and royalty alike; it shelters all workers, including fashion models, tycoons and yuppies; fabric is as visible in street fashion as in a designer boutique window. Fabric covers our chairs, our sofas, our beds, our windows, our floors and our walls. Fabric keeps us warm and also keeps us cool; it offers security, protection, elegance, sophistication, glamour, provocation, invitation, wit and luxury. It also indicates position or stature, wealth and ceremony. It creates a mood with color and texture, a mood quiet or exciting, sensuous, warm and comforting or cool and forbidding. No wonder we have a passion for fabrics.

Women, I think, have a natural affinity for fabrics. Maybe it goes back to civilization's beginnings, when

Jacket, *above*, and long sleeveless vest, *below*, designed from printed cotton designer panels, used in main body of both garments. Sleeves and side panels are cut and pieced from coordinating fabrics. Designed and made by the author; Porcella patterns. Michaele Vollbracht fabric.

A mix of fabrics are combined in a fascinating collage for this jacket, "Anything Goes," by Kim Masopust. Sleeves are knitted by Marlene Acosta. Photo by Richard Billings.

mothers wrapped their babies up like little cocoons in whatever was at hand. Maybe it comes too from the urge deep inside all of us to look as beautiful as possible while bowing to the primary function of clothes. The history of textiles is a fascinating one, for it is also the history of the world. I read just recently that Pakistan is supposed to be the birthplace of the textile industry and that the oldest known textile fragments were discovered in archeological excavations in the Indus Valley. Many of us have been fortunate enough to see ancient Peruvian textile fragments carefully preserved and exhibited, a small miracle indeed, since textiles are so fragile and so subject to time and climate.

We have access now to fabrics from all over the world, either hand or machine woven. They vary from coarse and nubby to smooth and shiny; from heavyweight to gossamer – it's enough to send your senses whirling. When you see such irresistible fabrics for sale, you'd better buy them while you have the chance; they won't be there when you go back. When I go into a fabric store, I don't see bolts and bolts of fabrics stacked against each other on the shelves. I see pitiful orphans, holding out their arms, begging me to take them home. How can anyone resist such a plea?

NATURAL AND SYNTHETIC FABRICS

Once upon a time we had only natural fabrics, cloth made from plants or animal hair or other such things. These are nature's own exquisite harvests, and happily we still have them. With the aid of technology, however, we also now have an amazing range of synthetics; they may be clones of the real thing, but they're pretty good clones. We've come a long way since the birth of polyester double-knit. Synthetics today have reached such a pinnacle that often the most expensive clothes are made from them; their fibers reinforce natural fibers for a dozen reasons, and they are similar in many ways to natural cloth. Both groups take color well, both offer a wide range of texture, most are easy to care for. Synthetics don't wrinkle, most are washable and they seldom need ironing. There is a trade-off, however, for they are not as comfortable in either hot or cold weather as natural fibers are. Synthetics are hot and clammy in summer and cold and clammy in winter, because the fibers don't breathe. Natural ones do, because they are living. There has been a happy compromise with many types of fabric, a blending of synthetic yarns with the natural ones to maintain the comfort of wearing along with reducing care to a minimum. Because of this, many natural fabrics are now "wrinkle free" and permanent press, features especially attractive to busy people.

We used to wear heavy woolens in the winter and thin cottons in the summer, but the thermal concept of clothes, so popular and necessary today, has changed our way of dressing, perhaps forever. We are able to attain maximum comfort by adding or subtracting layers, depending on the climate. This is a premise as invaluable to the traveller as to the working woman. Central heating and air conditioning have played a role, too. Layered dressing has not only been widely accepted but is being refined constantly.

Synthetics came into play when natural fibers were scarce and expensive. I remember how frustrating it was, especially for quilters who could not find all-cotton fabric in the shops. They settled for a 50/50 poly blend – if they were lucky – otherwise a 65/35. The fabric was thin and often the seams showed through. It was difficult to turn under a seam allowance and get it to stay there; the edges frayed constantly and the fabrics were almost impossible to press. Most of that has changed now. The cotton blends have improved, but they will never be as nice to work with as all-cotton. The silk look-alikes are wonderful; the colors and prints are vibrant and it's hard to tell the synthetic from the real thing.

GRAIN

Along with color, texture and fiber content, we need to consider the grain of fabric. This term refers to the woven threads and their direction. The warp threads, which run lengthwise in the fabric, are the strongest threads and they usually determine how a garment is cut, since grain determines the drape. If you look at your patterns, you'll find that each pattern

ABOVE & BELOW: Two jackets designed and made by the author from fabric yardage created by piecing assorted black and white fabrics.

GRAIN

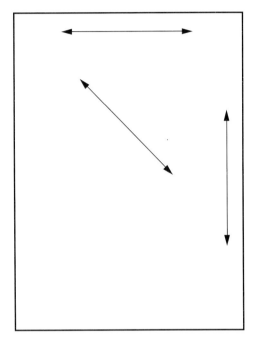

Grain lines for patterns and fabrics. Horizontal arrow is crosswise grain or woof; vertical arrow is lengthwise grain or warp; diagonal arrow is bias grain.

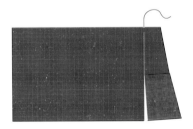

Straightening the end of fabric (crosswise grain) by pulling a thread, then cutting. You may also straighten the end of some fabrics by tearing.

After straightening crosswise grain, fold fabric horizontally and pin or baste raw edges and selvage edges together. If fabric does not lie flat when folded, dampen and pull diagonally, then press.

piece is marked with a grain line, a long line with a little arrow at each end. This indicates how the pattern piece is to be laid on the fabric; the grain line you see always refers to the lengthwise grain.

At right angles to the warp threads are the weft threads, and these establish the crosswise grain. There is a little more give in the crosswise than the lengthwise grain.

Now, if you fold the crosswise grain over to meet the lengthwise grain, (the two selvages run along the lengthwise grain), the fold in the fabric will be on the diagonal, the true bias. Bias has the most give and stretch of all. Even when you make a garment predominantly on the bias, the grain line of the pattern pieces will still be on the lengthwise grain. Several of the couture designers have mastered the art of working with bias and are known for their bias-cut garments.

Bias does not ravel, so you don't have to worry about seam finishes. You should stretch bias when you sew, otherwise the stitching may break.

Sometimes you may buy a fabric which has the design on only one side. This can be a luxury quality double-faced fabric, or it can be a fabric with a design printed on only one side and not woven in. This is true of many types of designs as well as plaids and checks. You'll never be able to straighten the design if it is printed off-grain, so check it carefully before purchase.

Often, cotton fabrics are wound on bolts off-grain; I'm sure you've bought plenty of these, for none of us has escaped. The fabric may be folded in the middle on the bolt, but the two selvages don't begin to meet; one side may be off by several inches. You can tell if you tear off some at the end to even the crosswise grain; you'll have a long long triangle with maybe a couple of inches at one end and almost nothing at the other. It is often very difficult to straighten the grain of fabric, but it's worth a try. Straighten one crosswise end, fold the fabric and match the selvages and pin the length of the fabric. Press damp, pulling diagonally as you work, and try to smooth out the wrinkles from the center fold. Every now and then I think I have straightened the grain without really washing the fabric and occasionally I have, but often, once the pins are removed, the fabric goes back to its original state.

If there are polyester or other synthetic threads mixed in with cottons, you may not be able to straighten the grain at all. On some garments, or in some patchwork, it may not make any difference, but you should check carefully before you spend the time working on a piece, for grain determines the hang of the garment and you don't want to end up with something that's lopsided.

COLOR

You can't think of fabric without thinking of color. As the song says, "You can't have one without the other." Color affects us emotionally and we gravitate toward the colors we like best. Whole careers are based on color studies, and art schools and art students devote much of their studies to the properties and interaction of colors. Many women in my classes have been despairing about their inability to use color and use it well; they are often filled with indecision, yet most women know a lot more about color than they think they do. You can learn a lot just by playing with fabrics.

Make a pile of scraps on your work table or on the floor and then step back and take a look. Squint. Take away some fabrics, add others and then look again. Put them with black, then put them with white, then put them with other shades of their own color family. The eye mixes color automatically and that eye is also easily trained. By just following such a simple exercise you can almost always come up with the right mix.

If you want to study color in depth, there are excellent books available; you can also learn a lot from a simple color wheel. These are found in art supply stores or stationery stores and they reduce color complexities to simple problems. They are all based, of course, on the primary colors, red, blue and yellow. The secondary colors are a mix of the primaries; if you add black to any of the mixes, you get a darker "value;" if you add white, you get a lighter "value." What I now know about color came from

Steve's birthday vest; a collage of personal mementos arranged on cotton fabric and covered with plastic. By the author.

Vest designed and made by the author from her "Simply Super Scrap Vest" pattern. Fabrics are cotton; prints from *Farmers' Almanac*, strips of a promotion fabric which reads "Never underestimate the power of a woman," and a cartoon-printed cotton are all combined in the vest.

working with it and from my own intuition. I can look at a mix of fabrics and tell if it's O.K. or not.

Many doctors and scientists, specifically in the behavioral and mental health areas, use color therapy with their patients. Pediatricians use it with babies and interior designers use it to create moods for both businesses and personal interiors. Perhaps you've had your colors "done." You find out – officially – which colors are most becoming to you and you are usually categorized in a season of the year. Amazingly, this seems to work very well, and if you follow the color range suggested, you'll look better and feel better about yourself.

Don't be afraid to mix colors or experiment with them. Put conflicting colors together; if they stay mad at each other, try a peacemaker in between. Once in a while, for a reason you'll never understand, you may buy something in a color you don't really like. I told you about my experience with that, but something else you might do (before you throw or give it away) is try to combine it with a color or colors you *do* like. It might just work! I can remember when "they" said brown and black wouldn't go together and neither would red and pink. How little "they" knew!

One of the smartest things you can do in building an interchangeable wardrobe is to pick two, perhaps three, main colors and stick with them. You can always add accents with scarves, bags, vests or an extra jacket. Several years ago I went to a seminar at Fashion Institute of Technology in New York. The seminar featured Michaele Vollbracht, a well known designer, and he talked about getting started in the fashion world. He showed us most of the garments from that first collection and they were all in red, black and white. There was sportswear and evening wear and clothes in between, but all in the same three colors. He laughed when he told us about it. He said he was criticized for not broadening his color field, but then he said: "I had very little money to launch myself. It seemed to me much smarter to buy three colors and swing a memorable show than buy a little of several colors and end up with a hodge-podge." What good advice....

Yellow is a bright and beckoning color, the color

of sun and the color of many flowers. It's a strong color, and the eye tends to seek it out. You need to be careful about using too much because of its dominant quality, yet there are times when you feel you can't get enough of it. Blue is quieter, calm and soothing most of the time, but strong and electric other times. Red is a power color, a stop-in-your-tracks color; it commands attention, and people pay attention to it. Bill Blass says, "When in doubt, wear red. It always stands out in a room full of people." Diana Vreeland was another advocate of red and so is William Accorsi, who carves wonderful puzzles and toys and sculptures. Accorsi said:

"The first color is red. Red was invented by a Spaniard who was a chemist and as a hobby did bull fighting. He used it on his cape and got bulls madder than anyone else. The second color is blue – blue was found lying around on the ground by Mr. DaVinci when he was searching for purple. Another color is yellow. No one knows who really discovered yellow. Red-yellow-blue. I think that is about it except for black and white." (From Accorsi Puzzles; quoted with permission.) I agree with him. The first color for me is red, too.

TEXTURE

Texture is another characteristic of fabric, almost as important as color. It refers to weave. The weave may be rough, nubby or smooth; it may be loose or tight. It may be uneven, or it may have a nap; it may be ribbed or plain. Cloth has an irresistible tactile appeal; your hand automatically reaches out to feel, to rub, to caress, to pinch or pull or play with it. A swatch of red satin is shiny and reflects the light. A swatch of red velvet is dense and deep, and it absorbs the light. Loosely woven fabric drapes better than a crisp, tightly woven one. Napped fabrics change with the light. For a good all-over look, you cut and sew everything with the nap running in the same direction. If you change the direction of the nap in the same garment, it will look like you have used two different fabrics, and this can add variety and excitement with little effort and expense. A contrast in textures is always exciting in your work, and later on,

"Eat Your Heart Out, John Malloy" coat created entirely from red neckties in a striking combination of pattern. By Rosalind Ward. Photo courtesy Fairfield Processing Corp.

you'll find out how to create textures of your own.

Weight differs with fabric, from sheer, gossamer wisps of cloth to heavy and sturdy tweeds. There is a lot in between, with light and medium weights predominating. Many of these can be combined successfully, depending on the pattern or design. A velvet dress could have a chiffon yoke. A tweed jacket could be trimmed with silk appliques; flannel can be combined with lamé. Even unlikely combinations, "odd couples," often work when you least expect it.

WOOL

Most of our wool is from sheep. Some more esoteric wools come from camels and llama and goats; I have a friend who spins and weaves dog hair and knits wonderful hats from it. Wools are comfortable to wear in almost any season; they wrinkle very little and are wonderful travel companions. Finishes come from woolly to crisp, and weights from heavy through medium and light to gossamer. There is also a pile finish or napped finish. Tweeds are rough and irregular, either in wool or silk. Melton cloth is a medium heavy wool used for outerwear. Flannels are smooth and matte finished and available in marvelous colors. Menswear suitings, also know as worsteds, are lightweight and crisp and tailor beautifully; they hold pleats well too. Wool crepes are soft and nubby, almost pebble-like. Gabardine is crisp, smooth and conservative; it has a fine rib that you have to look at closely to see. Wool jersey is a single knit, a supple lightweight wool that is comfortable to wear and almost wrinkle free. Double wool knits are heavier and used for suits or coats. Both wool lace and wool challis are soft thin wools which drape beautifully. Wool challis is noted for its rich and colorful prints, one of which is paisley.

Alpaca and mohair woolens are soft, warm and fluffy. Unlined, they make wonderful ponchos, coats or capes. Lambswool may also be used for outerwear and it is also used as a thin layer of interlining.

Many wools are hand washable, but it's a good idea to test-wash first. Most wools we buy are preshrunk before we buy them, but it's a good idea to ask and be sure. Since pressing is such an important part of a garment's appearance, it's better to have your work dry-cleaned so it can also be professionally pressed. A simple wool garment could probably be washed successfully, in tepid water with mild soap – Ivory® liquid, Ensure® or Woolite®. The important thing is to keep the water temperature constant, for it's the change in temperature that causes shrinkage.

You can, of course, shrink wool deliberately to make your own "boiled" wool. The fibers condense and mat together and finally have a thick, felted appearance. This type of fabric made the Geiger jackets famous.

SILK

Silk is another natural fabric, available from the sheerest chiffons to heavy tweeds. It's produced from the protein filament that *Bobyx mori* moths spin when they are working on a new cocoon. Silk has a luxurious hand and like wool, is available in many weights and weaves. It takes color well, but some colors may bleed when silk is washed. Some years ago Vogue published some guidelines about silk in their pattern magazine. They advocated washing many silks because the washing process actually rejuvenated the fibers and added natural sizing. They pointed out too that only warm water should be used, and a mild soap or shampoo, but no detergent.

Chiffons, organza, gauze, georgette and silk lace are all wonderfully thin, transparent luxury fabrics. China and palace silks are a little heavier; silk linen is crisp for tailored wear. Broadcloth is smooth and comes in a wide range of colors. Silk noil, sometimes called raw silk, is wonderful to work with. It looks a little like cotton, with a nubby weave and a good weight. It takes color well and it also can be washed successfully. You can use it alone or combine it with other fabrics. Silk crepes are luxury fabrics; they come in brilliant colors, they're soft and pliable and they drape well. Silk satins come in several weights; their sheen makes them particularly desirable for evening wear. The crepes and satins both have a tendency to fray, as do the silk velvets, so seams must

"Daddy's Ties," a stunning outfit by Shirley Botsford, created from her father's neckties. Ties are separated with black lace insertion strips; a fitted bodice complements the very full skirt and creates a marvelous mix of pattern. Photo courtesy Fairfield Processing Corp.

"Orient Express," a haori coat of Skinner Ultra-suede® fabric. Pieced, appliqued, quilted with single and double needle stitching. Sleeves are interchangable and detachable. Designed and made by the author.

you're ready to go. It may be re-embroidered or beaded, even worn for sports and on the beach, so take another look at that lace tablecloth or crocheted bedspread.

A touch of glitz in your piecing or applique could give your garment a special spark. There are wonderful lamés and metallic fabrics around, in many colors as well as gold and silver and bronze. The ones with the knitted backing are easier to sew than the woven ones, because of the fraying. If you do sew with woven metallics, use a featherweight bias press-on interfacing with them.

Felt, especially wool felt, is a great fabric for outerwear; it doesn't necessarily have to be lined and you can decorate it to your heart's content. You do not have to finish the raw edges at all, which makes finishing easier and faster. Don't forget Ultrasuede® and Facile® fabric, both produced by Skinner. Ultrasuede® is the suede look-alike, easy to sew and washable – in fact, it looks better after washing, I think. The kid sister is Facile®, lighter weight and a softer version but with the same color range. There are other fake suedes and leathers on the market which can be used alone or combined with other fabrics. The real suedes are popular too, as are leathers, and now that they come in garment weight they are as easy to sew as cottons. Stenciled calfskin can look like any exotic leather, including snakeskin. There are also the vinyl look-alikes. I use a regular sewing needle for these; I think the wedge-shaped leather needle makes too big a hole.

There are fraudulent furs as well as fraudulent leathers, and even a little fur here and there works beautifully with patchwork.

Handwoven cottons from Guatemala and Mexico are of medium weight, have a good hand and come in a fine color range. These are wonderful fabrics, in wonderful colors and patterns. I do not recommend washing them, however, as the colors bleed. Indian saris in both cotton and silk will give you a six or seven yard strip of fine fabric, often with metallic or *real* gold (for a price) and silver borders.

Aside from yardage, you'll have bits and pieces and odds and ends in your fabric stash. Don't forget quilt blocks or unfinished quilt tops or even a good section from a worn quilt. I'm for recycling whenever possible. Tag sales and flea markets are the best bets for these, for antique shops have inflated prices. Lastly, don't forget pre-quilted fabric. It's a great time saver, and some of it is really good looking. You can also add to the quilting before you use it and change its appearance completely.

FABRICS: SURFACE DESIGN

This is sometimes called gilding the lily. You may have a wonderful selection or stash of fabrics on hand (most of us do), but of course you never have quite enough. There is an elusive color you can't find and there is always a new print or plaid to see and buy. You may also want to experiment a little – or a lot – and create some colors or designs of your own with paint or dye. You can stencil, silk screen, rubber stamp or write on your fabric with a permanent pen and you'll probably have a marvelous time. I can only tell you a little about the experiences I've had; if you want to pursue any of these in depth and seriously, there are some fine instruction books which cover almost everything and any good art supply store should have a selection of them, as well as the paints and other materials you'll need. You can overdye fabric to give it an antique look and you can use a Clorox® solution to remove some color, thus creating a new design.

FABRIC PAINTING

My experience with fabric painting is on the beginner level, but I've had a good time with it. I use the Deka® paints. They have good color, the paint dries quickly, you can clean up with water, and you can set the color with an iron – those are reasons enough for me. Be sure your fabric is free of sizing; wash it first if you're in doubt. I try to keep things simple and cheap. My brushes come from the dime store, but I also use bits of sponge or anything that might give me more texture. The brushes range from 3" to 4" wide to a small brush for details (just in case). I do my painting in the laundry room, with a sheet of plywood laid over the washer and dryer for a working surface.

White cotton jacket painted by Heather Avery in designs inspired by Bible images. Collection of the author.

Cover the plywood with a plastic drop cloth or whatever you have, then lay your fabric on this. I use foil pans for mixing colors and just start painting, usually without any design in mind. You can do as much or as little as you like. When you work with dry fabric, your brush strokes will show more and it will take more paint to cover the surface. When you've finished and the fabric is dry, you can heat-set it; before you do this, you could add some spatter painting on top of the brush painting. The easiest way to do this is to put your paint in a little plastic squeeze bottle and then squirt it on the fabric at random. You can also put the paint in a spray bottle and try that too; your paint must be thinned enough to go through the nozzle.

When I paint wet, I wet the fabric thoroughly, then spread it out on the plastic-covered plywood. The brush strokes will run into each other and give you a soft, watercolor effect, and you'll also get some nice color changes and transparencies. You can let the fabric dry as is or squish it together, wadded up, and let it dry that way. You get some interesting designs that way. Take a piece of sponge and dip it in paint, then apply it wherever you want to; this could give you an extra color accent. A stippled design looks good too, but it can be pretty messy. Get paint on your brush, and then, holding it over the fabric, hit the brush with a ruler or stick so the paint spatters over the fabric. I spattered the laundry the last time I did this, so I try to be more careful now.

Sometime, when you've painted on a length of wet fabric, lay a length of dry fabric on top of it and press the two together; you'll get a duplicate pattern on the dry piece, though it may be fainter.

When I was growing up, my girl friends all made broom-stick skirts and of course I couldn't be left out, so I made one too. Maybe you did also. We wrapped fabric around a broomstick, pulling it into pleats and folds, tied it in place, then dyed it with Rit. You can do the same thing with paints. Fasten your fabric tightly to the pole or stick and pull it down in pleats or gathers then tie it securely in two or three places. You can do this with either wet or dry fabric; I think wet works better, and also, the pleats will stay longer. Now take your brush, dip it in paint and apply it either in horizontal or vertical stripes. They'll be uneven, of course, and run into each other, but the effect will be good. Let the fabric dry on the pole. This technique is similar in some ways to the "wet and wrinkled" technique you'll read about (and do) in the TRICKS AND TREATS section.

You can also spot paint fabric, add your own color accents to an already painted fabric. As I mentioned earlier, once you've finished painting, you need to heat-set your design. Put the fabric right side up on the ironing board, with a presscloth over it. Use a fairly hot DRY iron and go over it a couple of times to be sure it "takes." Remove the presscloth for the final ironing, press for a couple of minutes and your masterpiece should be permanently set.

FABRIC DYEING

Fabric dyeing has turned out to be quite an art – so has fabric painting, especially when both are done by dedicated and knowledgeable people. Again, my dyeing experience is on the beginner level. I've used Rit® in the washing machine or a large tub – following directions. I've also done some tea and coffee dyeing. The health hazards of dyeing discouraged me from pursuing it above the simplest levels, but I also find that the colors I want or need are almost always available in commercial fabrics. In recent years too, many women have set themselves up in small businesses by dyeing fabric and marketing it; usually the vendor area in any quilt conference has two or three booths where such fabrics are available, and some are also available by mail. The same holds true for silk-screened fabrics, and hand-screened prints can also be purchased.

You can over-dye a fabric and perhaps give it a new lease on life. The base color will change and you may be in for some delightful surprises. Tea or coffee dyeing adds a creamy tinge to otherwise white fabric, and it's possible to get several shades from beige to tan, depending on the strength of the tea or coffee.

QUICK PIECING

This is one of the design elements I'm talking about: you probably already know how to do this, yet there may be newcomers to the field who have never heard of it, so here goes. The technique was first introduced by Barbara Johannah in her book *Quick Quilting*. I thought the idea was wonderful, but felt that I could simplify it, so I devised my own diagram and steps. This method of quick piecing, illustrated at right, gives you a two-triangle square without cutting the triangles out individually, then sewing them together. You could easily put together a whole garment – or a whole quilt top – using this technique, perhaps changing colors and scale to add interest. I like to make these squares ahead of time, perhaps in different sizes and different color combinations, and have them ready to use when I need them.

CHECKERBOARD PIECING

Many pieced or strip designs are offshoots of Seminole piecing and this is one of them. Decide on the finished size of your checkerboards, then add the two seam allowances of ¼" each and cut strips of fabric. Sew two contrasting strips together and press. Cut into segments the same size as the width to form a strip of squares. Now alternate the segments to form a checkerboard and stitch together, matching seams. A third "layer" of segments will make a 9-patch or you can keep on going for as long a strip or big a block as you like. This is also something you can do ahead of time when you are designing a garment.

STRIP PIECING

Strip piecing covers such a large area I could not possibly mention all the possibilities. In fact, there are several books on the market dealing with this one subject alone. It is such a popular technique I feel sure you already know a lot about it, so we can cover just the main points.

Strip piecing can be straight or curved and usually it refers to strips of equal width, although this is subject to change. Straight grain strips should be cut on the crosswise grain of your fabric, although there isn't any law that says you must follow this rule. Cross-

QUICK PIECING

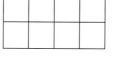

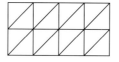

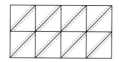

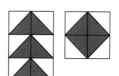

DIAGRAM 1. Select two fabrics. On the wrong side of one, draw a grid for the size square you've chosen. For instance, a 2" square needs a 2½" grid; a 2½" square needs a 3" grid.

DIAGRAM 2. Draw diagonal lines through the grid in one direction only. Place your two fabrics together, right sides facing, and pin securely.

DIAGRAM 3. Machine stitch ¼" on both sides of diagonal line. Lift needle when crossing horizontal lines so corners of squares are not sewed together.

DIAGRAM 4. Cut on horizontal lines of grid to form strips, then cut on vertical lines to form squares. Next, cut on the diagonal line, between the stitched lines to form triangles. Open the triangles out into a square and press. Play with these squares, forming a design, then stitch together.

CHECKERBOARD PIECING

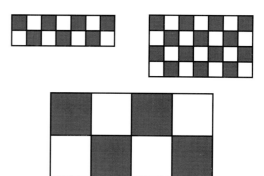

"Navigational Lights," a pieced silk and cotton coat by Cheryl Trostrud-White.

"Magic Kimono" by Tracy Stilwell. The shell is pieced of assorted fabrics. Inside, the lining records Tracy's thoughts, observations and affirmations.

grain is easier to work with and if you cut into the full width, you have strips 45" long. These can be cut with shears or a rotary cutter, whichever is more comfortable for you to use. I usually test fabric to see if it tears O.K., too, and if so, I often tear my strips, for they tear on the true crossgrain and it is completely accurate. In testing, if the edges stretch or the fabric for any reason isn't easy to tear, don't try it.

In planning a strip-pieced design for a garment, you'll need to make some decisions before you start. First, choose fabrics and colors you want to use. Second, do you want to strip piece the entire garment or just sections of it? Do you want all the strips the same width or do you want to vary them? Often, it's hard to pin-point all of this ahead of time, for design has a way of unfolding and developing as you work. It helps, however, if you cut strips, a lot of strips, at the beginning, then you have something ready to help you plan. I usually cut strips of varying widths, but I also sew some of them into bands, for I like the accent of seam or strip inserts in a garment. As you know, most piecing is easier if you work on a foundation or base. Either muslin or flannel, pre-shrunk, are fine. Sometimes I use a thin batt, like Cotton Classic®, but the fabric is a better stabilizer. Or, if I want to add a layer of batting and perhaps do some quilting later, I use a thin batiste for a base fabric or even strip on paper, then tear the paper away later.

If you have pre-cut strips, some quick-pieced squares and some checkerboards on hand, you have a head-start on a pieced design. Lay the foundation sections out on your work table, then arrange the design on top of them. Change them around until you are happy with them, then begin to sew. Your ideas still may change as the garment takes shape, but that's half the fun of it – and even you may be surprised at the way it turns out!

If you want to strip piece yardage rather than work with individual pattern pieces, don't use a foundation; just sew the strips together in the color sequence you've chosen, press the seams and you're then ready to lay your pattern pieces on top and cut. Sometimes this is a good way to use up your ugly fabrics (why did I ever buy *that*? What did I see in *that*?), working them into strip-pieced fabrics; you may find they change character completely when surrounded by other colors and patterns. At least, it's worth a try. You don't need to concentrate entirely on solids; a mix often makes fabric more interesting. Large scale prints, checks and stripes and plaids and polka dots can be incorporated into the strip piecing; you'll find it endlessly fascinating.

SEMINOLE PIECING

This technique originated, of course, with the Seminole Indians. The designs created from this intricate and precise way of piecing have symbolic and religious meaning for the Indians. We use the designs in a purely decorative way. Even a little bit of Seminole work used in a jacket or vest gives it a spark. The piecing can be very simple or it can be a complex geometric pattern. (See the diagrams at right). Cheryl Bradkin, well known in the quilt world for her Seminole piecing, wrote a very good book about it. The book has been out of print for awhile, but should be available again by the time you read this.

STRING PIECING

There is very little difference between strip and string piecing. "String" piecing is an "old-timey" description; it refers to the strip or "strings" leftover when fabric was straightened or a garment cut out. Most of these strings, as they are called, were narrow and irregular, too narrow to use alone, so they were stitched to another and another until the pieced fabric was big enough to use in another project. Usually paper was used to stabilize the stitching; it was easier to handle the narrow strips this way. We think of strip piecing as being composed of strips of uniform width, no matter the width, but the line of definition between strip and string piecing is very faint. Paper or fabric as a foundation can be used for either technique, although it is almost always used for string piecing. String piecing is associated too with thriftiness or frugality; it started at a time when every little piece of cloth was treasured and nothing was thrown away.

Afro-American piecing is often based on the string

BASIC SEMINOLE PIECING

DIAGRAM 1. Contrasting fabric strips are seamed together to make a band.

DIAGRAM 2. Band is cut apart in segments. This is called a "straight cut."

DIAGRAM 3. Cuts are seamed together, offset or staggered by width of fabric strip.

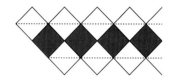

DIAGRAM 4. The completed Seminole design ready to be joined to plain strips on either side. Dotted lines in diagram are sewing lines.

DIAGRAM 5. Original band, now cut at an angle instead of straight.

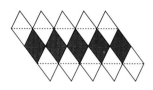

DIAGRAM 6. Angle cuts seamed together, offset by one fabric strip. This design creates an elongated diamond pattern.

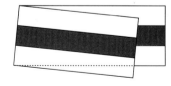

DIAGRAM 7. Original band again, this time folded in half for cutting a mirror-image design.

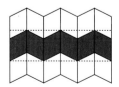

DIAGRAM 8. Cuts are alternated as they are seamed, to form the Seminole mirror-image. Also called herringbone or zigzag.

A jacket pieced of squares and rectangles of Thai silk. Satin ribbon stitched over each seam. By the author.

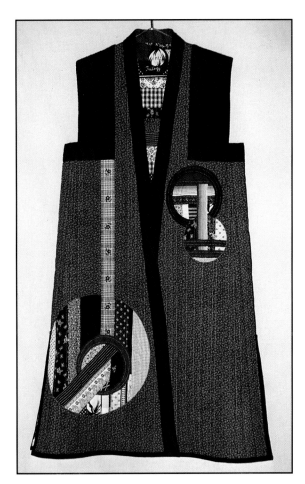

"Trilogy" by Shirley Fomby. Long sleeveless coat pieced of three fabrics, three colors and three design elements.

piecing principle; the interesting effects achieved come from the irregularities in size and the mix of colors. The technique was used primarily in Afro-American quilts rather than clothing. I still think of strings as wedge-shaped, as stretched-out triangles as long as the widths of the fabric. The original purpose of sewing them all together was to make a piece of fabric large enough to be a block or shape.

RANDOM PIECING

This is a description I use for pieced fabric yardage which doesn't fit into any other category. It can be made up of strips, squares, rectangles, triangles or any geometric shape and it is essentially scrap fabric yardage. Try for a mix of lights and darks and don't worry about points or corners matching. It resembles crazy patchwork a little bit, but you don't need a foundation or base fabric for it. If you have to, trim the scraps a little so that you have only straight seaming; it's easier.

CURVED SEAM PIECING

Curved seam piecing is a happy change from the discipline of straight lines; it has a softer look. Stitching curved seams, however, requires more precision than straight ones, and you will need a pattern for your design. To get started, draw your curved design on the paper pattern. Now lay blank newsprint or shelf paper or heavy tracing paper over the marked pattern. You should be able to see through the paper well enough to trace it. Trace the pattern outline, too, and when finished, cut out so that you have a duplicate pattern piece for each section of your garment.

Number the curved seam sections on the original paper pattern, then copy the numbers on the duplicate. You will cut the duplicate apart and use the sections as templates, but before you do this, be sure to

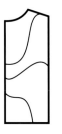
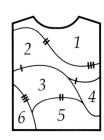

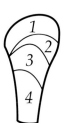

mark the seams with cross-hatches so you will know where to join or match the seams. The numbers on the curved sections will help you with place-ment after the pieces are cut out, for they will corre-spond with the numbered pieces on the master pat-tern.

Cut out the templates. They are the finished size, so when you cut them from fabric you must add ¼" seam allowance – carefully measured. Precision is important. Transfer the cross-hatch marks to the out-side edge so seams will match; they should fit together perfectly. Press the seams to one side. Shal-low and gentle curves are quite easy to do, but you have to be a little more careful with deep inside and outside, concave and convex, curves. Staystitch the curves on the ¼" seam line, or one thread outside, then clip through the seam allowance almost to the stitching line. The clips in the inside curve will release the fabric and help your work to lie flat. The clips in the outside curve will overlap instead of pleat and also keep your work flat. The clips are easier than notching in the outside curve.

You can draw curved designs freehand or use an architect's flexible curve, available at an art supply store. I first learned to use these for landscapes in pictorial quilts, then found they work equally well for garment design. These curves come in several sizes or lengths and are ½" thick at the base. This works fine, since our seams are ¼". Bend the curve into the shape you want and it will stay put until you change it again. Shallow or gentle curves are easier to piece than deeper ones. To use this flexible curve, lay it on the fabric you've chosen and trace around the top edge of the curve. On the second piece of fabric, which will be sewed to the first, lay the flexible curve down and trace the bottom edge of the curve; you then have your two ¼" seam allowances built in ready to sew.

I want to add a last reminder when sewing curved seams; any time you cut a curve into fabric, you are cutting on the bias grain. There is natural stretch here and unless your curves are very deep, you may not have to clip the seams; the stretch will accommodate the curves.

"Heathcote Revisited" by the author. Using five shades of velveteen, one sleeve is pieced in shallow horizontal curves, the other in vertical curves. Seams are piped in gold. Photo courtesy of *Needle and Thread* magazine.

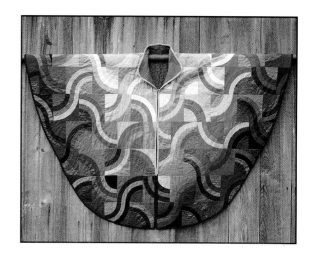

"Indiana Farmlands at 30,000 Feet" by Anita Hardwick. Curved seam piecing with 6" blocks as a base for this prize-winning cape.

Front view of jacket by Jo Ann Lopez. Bias piecing at its best.

BIAS PIECING

We're all familiar with straight seam and curved seam piecing and in fact use many other piecing techniques to bring interest to our work. What is less well known in the piecing category is bias patchwork or "diagonal piecing." I first saw this used in a most effective way on jackets JoAnn Lopez had made; later, when I talked to her about it, she very graciously permitted me to include her technique in this book, so you have a treat in store for you. It is something worth pursuing.

JoAnn is a West Coast production artist who creates stunning garments which are sold in boutiques and specialty shops. JoAnn's garments are noted for her innovative designs and excellent workmanship. The bias patchwork is her trademark.

She prefers to use ethnic fabrics in her work; heavier Guatemalan and Mexican cottons, heavy silks from India and Thailand. Her garments are pieced but not quilted and because of the weight of the fabric, they hang beautifully. She chooses her color groups from a focal or center piece, perhaps a stunning embroidery or a special woven design. She "pulls" colors from this, using four or five fabrics from each color family, from solid colors to stripes, checks and plaids. Often she uses Guatemalan belts or sections of Japanese country obis in her work. The color families are sewed together in wide strips to create yardage, so that she might have blues running into reds running into purples running into greens, with another color accent along the way. She also has, of course, the main fabric for the garment, almost always a solid color. The yardage she stitches together is the basis for patchwork.

When she has enough pieced yardage, JoAnn presses it and lays it flat on her worktable, then, with an architect's right-angle triangle, marks a true bias. She cuts strips 1½" to 2" wide for piecing and she measures often to be sure the strips are accurate. She then tears batiste into strips of equal width on straight grain to be used as backing for the bias and presses the two together, wrong side facing. The pressing holds the two layers in place and the straight grain of the batiste will help stabilize the sewing when she stitches bias strips into her work.

These strips of bias patchwork are inserted between strips of the main garment fabric, although occasionally she will chevron two strips for another type design. Sometimes the strips go the entire length of the garment and at other times they are staggered into different lengths. Sometimes too, JoAnn faces the end of a bias strip and lets it hang free instead of stitching it firmly in place.

This might be a little intimidating for someone trying it for the first time, but it is an exciting challenge well worth the effort. JoAnn says one of the things which helps her in the beginning is to stack the straight strips together, separating them by color in the sequence she plans to use. When she is ready to piece yardage, she can then pick a strip from each stack, working her way down the line; this establishes a rhythm of color.

AFRICAN PIECING

This type of piecing, to me, is almost like jazz, for there is so much improvising. In recent years, patchwork clothing and quilts of Afro-American origin have been "discovered." Of course they were there all along, but we just weren't aware of them. There is a freshness and a naiveté about this type of patchwork, an air of joyous abandon. Many Afro-Americans do not bother with measurements; there is no need for them to fortify themselves with rulers and rotary cutters. Often, they use scraps, uncut and untrimmed, and fit them in with the rest. If there is trimming to be done, it is done without benefit of tape measure and there is always an element of surprise. Afro-Americans have been the greatest users of string piecing and this element of thrift carries over into all their work. You can get effects similar to African piecing by sorting through your scraps, aligning the colors and starting to sew, either on a paper foundation or without it. It might be a kind of modern crazy patch.

Kente cloth is a product of Africa, made of sewing together the 4" strips hand woven by men on small looms. The yardage thus created is used for clothing, loose, toga-like garments. Today, good Kente cloth is a collector's dream, very expensive because of the time involved. Using the Kente cloth as an idea, we might look through our fabrics and select a few which could be used in a similar way; 4" strips cut, then joined in whatever color sequence we chose. You also might create a similar fabric by seaming together strips of the same fabric and using a piping to accent the seams.

In patchwork of Central Asia, there seems to be the same disregard for precision as in the work of the Afro-Americans. I have seen patchwork of ikats, which were cut up then sewed together in panels or strips, with no thought to aligning either size or pattern. We so often expect to see a repeat or rhythm in our fabric and it's rather refreshing to find such abandon in piecework.

AFGHANI PATCHWORK

This patchwork, which somewhat bears a resemblance to our flying geese pattern on a smaller scale, was used to accent many of the Afghani garments. Yvonne Porcella discovered it on some of the ethnic clothes she collected, and she developed the technique for using it. Some of the examples were only ¼" wide, which might be inspiration to work toward, but Yvonne scaled hers to 1½" and sometimes even that seems small! The original patchwork comes from the Uzbek region of northern Afghanistan and is done by nomadic peoples.

I used a strip of Afghani patchwork across the front of my tunic "New York State of Mind" (see page 72) and Ardis James used it along one side of the front in her long vest (page 36). Size and color combinations are up to you. You work with an equilateral triangle and bars or strips half the width of the triangle. I often do strips of this by hand – it is my airport work. I put everything I need – fabric scraps, plastic templates, needle, thread, scissors and thimble in a plastic envelope to carry with me. With this to occupy my time, I don't mind waiting in airports.

Yvonne sent me the instructions and diagrams, included on the opposite page, and very graciously said I might pass them on to you, so here they are. In the photo to the left, you can see how the strip looks while you are working on it. The foundation strip with a pencil line down the center is also visible.

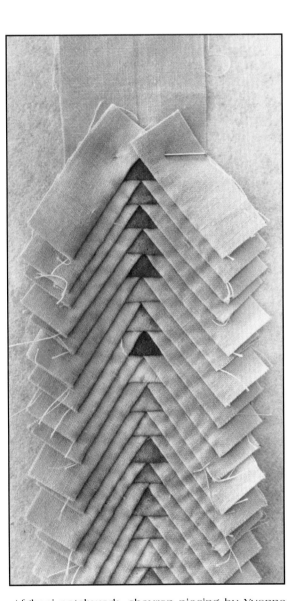

Afghani patchwork, chevron piecing by Yvonne Porcella. Photo: Karen Drellich.

CHEVRON PIECING INSTRUCTIONS

Courtesy of Yvonne Porcella

For best results, sew by hand.

Three elements:
1. Foundation strip ½" wide by 45" long. Can be shorter. Foundation fabric should be lightweight cotton. Draw a line down center, marking width of piece in half.
2. 1½" equilateral triangles (measuring 1½" tip to tip)
3. Bars cut ¾" wide by 2½" long.

Place first triangle down right-side up on lower edge of foundation. Tip of triangle lines up with drawn line.

Step 1.
Right sides together, sew bar using ¼" seam allowance, along the right edge of triangle. Top edge of bar meets tip of triangle. End of bar will overlap foundation. Turn bar right side up and finger press bar.

Step 2.
Place another bar right sides together on left edge of triangle. Sew with ¼" seam. Turn bar right side up and finger press.

Step 3.
Place 2nd triangle, right sides together, on top of work. ¼" seam allowance across base of triangle lines up with the top of past triangle. Sew base of 2nd triangle then fold triangle up, right side up and line tip of triangle up with line drawn on foundation.

Continue with Steps 1 and 2, etc.

Finished strip can be trimmed to 2" wide, and when sewn into work will be 1¼" wide finished.

Use ¼" wide masking tape if desired to mark seams while hand sewing. Tape is easily removed and will last about 10 uses.

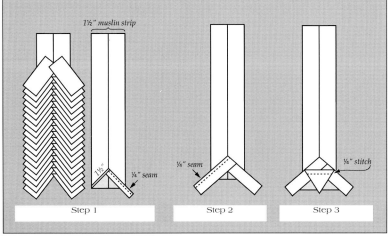

1½" muslin strip

1½"   ¼" seam

¼" seam   ¼" stitch

| Step 1 | Step 2 | Step 3 |

ABOVE: "New York State of Mind" by the author. Note strip of Afghani piecing diagonally across front.

BELOW: Back view of "New York State of Mind."

"City Lights" by the author. Strip-pieced jacket of cottons and lamé. Porcella pattern.

PATCHWORK

A diagram of Japanese 16th century patchwork, adapted for modern day piecing. Strips could be from 4 to 8" wide and a variety of fabrics used. Join strips edge to edge, or use a narrow solid strip between, or use piping.

JAPANESE SIXTEENTH CENTURY PATCHWORK

A study of Japanese Noh costumes and their kosodes, is enough to excite anyone's imagination. Not only are the fabrics exquisite, but much of the patchwork has a very contemporary look; it is hard to believe it was done so many hundreds of years ago. We've been able to adapt much of it into our patchwork dictionary, for the geometric shapes, the hexagon, the wide diamond and the clamshell are all universal; they don't belong to any one place or time. Many of the Japanese kimonos use the diamond and hexagon motif, and often the hexagon is shown with a center seam. We use the clamshell in patchwork, but in addition, we use it also as a quilting design.

I have a book called *Japanese Costume and Textile Arts* by Seiroku Noma, published jointly by Weatherhill of New York and Heibonsha of Tokyo. In it are two color plates, one of a kosode and one of a dofuko. The kosode (see figure on opposite page) fabric is described as tie-dyed, but it looks for all the world like sophisticated piecing. It dates from the second half of the 16th century. The dofuko is a patchwork of gold and silver brocades and damask from the Muromachi period, about 1560. Again, it is a stunning example of patchwork which can be readily translated into modern use. It is interesting to find that patchwork or piecing was commonly found in garments of such an early period and had risen to such artistic heights.

Much of the early patchwork followed precise rules. One such piece I saw in an exhibit was constructed from parts of Noh costumes, pieced together into a Buddhist priest's robe following rigid rules of assembly. The pattern of piecing was supposed to symbolize the vows of poverty and humility of the Buddhist priests. Completed with such elegant and sumptuous fabrics, there was a certain paradox to it, yet the fabrics were visually very exciting when contained in such a simple patchwork grid.

I worked out a 16th century piecing grid which could fit into our current piecing techniques and following is a diagram of it. You may want to use the diagram above as a guide, modifying it for the variety of fabrics you are using. Work with foundation strips of muslin or flannel. These can be any width, from 4"

BAZAAR BIRDS AND BEASTS, back view: award-winning jacket by the author of handwoven Guatemalan cotton. Silk, cotton and lamé applique embellished with hand and machine embroidery, beads and shi-shas. Fasteners are muñecas, Guatemalan folk dolls. Made for Bazaar del Mundo fashion fair.

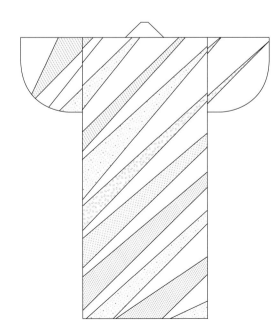

Drawing of a Japanese kosode, dating from the second half of the 16th century. This could be adapted easily into modern day piecing for a garment.

Patchwork Dofuko made for a famous Japanese general, Uesugu Kenshin, about 1560. Seventeen kinds of rare Chinese brocades were used.

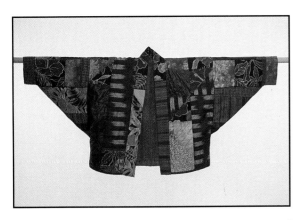

Pieced jacket by the author. An adaptation of Japanese 16th century patchwork.

to 8". Stitch and flip the fabrics until the strip is covered. The diagram indicates a variety of shapes and placement and it is only intended to give you an idea of how to follow through, but the piecing is simple and you won't have any trouble with it. When you are finished, the strips can be joined edge to edge or you can separate them with a narrow strip of solid color or a strip of piping.

PRE-PIECED DESIGNS AND QUILT BLOCKS

Quiltmaking and garment making are so closely intertwined that often the techniques and approaches, fabrics and colors we use in one can easily be transferred to the other. Years ago, when "wearable art" first began to surface, strip-pieced vests and log-cabin jackets were ubiquitous. Maybe they still are, but they are far more sophisticated now than the earlier efforts. I've talked earlier about getting ideas and inspiration for garments, but another suggestion you might consider is using quilt blocks or parts of blocks, in your garment. Perhaps you made up some blocks of a pattern you liked; perhaps you started a quilt you never finished or perhaps you have some blocks you picked up at a flea market. Often such little goodies can slip right in with other types of piecing and add an interesting design to your garment. Try one in a shoulder area or perhaps on a sleeve, cut it in half or slice a corner or two off it. An irregular shape is often more interesting than a square, and speaking of squares, when you are working on garments, a square placed on point will

"Blue Ice" by Kim Masopust. Kim uses the familiar Log Cabin pattern in an unfamiliar way.

PRE-PIECED DESIGNS AND QUILT BLOCKS

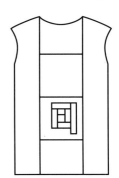
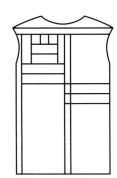

Possible placements for Log Cabin or other quilt blocks as basis or focal point for pieced design.

be far more flattering than one used as is. Fragments of blocks can be framed with pieced strips or inserted as a repeat in several different places.

If you have no ready-made blocks or don't want to use them, flip through a quilt pattern book and look at some of the diagrams. This is a good way to get ideas for pieced designs. Remember, even a section of it will do – you may not need the whole block.

One-patch patterns are good designs, too, and most of them are easy and can be machine pieced. The hexagon, triangle or wide diamond are probably the most popular. Think of Flying Geese or A Thousand Pyramids when you think of triangles and the Baby Block pattern when you think of wide diamonds. The Brick quilt pattern is another one which could easily be used and any of these could be planned with two or three colors, or used together scrap fashion.

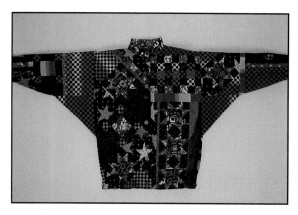

"California Neon" by Janet Paluch. Using shocking pink, chartreuse green and flagman orange, Janet created a parody on California neon fabrics. The piecing is based on a 6" Variable Star block quilt pattern.

Silk jacket by Donna Wilder, pieced in Tumbling Blocks design using the wide diamond as a one-patch geometric template.

Ellyn Mosbarger's lovely evening outfit of polyester crepe, satin and net, embellished with sheer appliques.

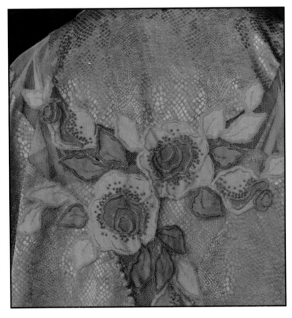

A detail of Ellyn Mosbarger's organdy applique for sheer fabrics; Ellyn used the turn-under-and-sew-as-you-go method.

APPLIQUE:
Don't leave home without it

Applique, unfortunately, has never been as popular as piecing. Many people think it is more difficult, but this simply is not true. It is different, but it is not more difficult. It may be the most potentially decorative form of needlework or sewing, since it is entirely free of technical limitations. You don't have to cope with the discipline of matching all the corners and seams and keeping the stitching line absolutely straight. You may experience far less wear and tear; applique is restful and it is also exciting.

We need inspiration for applique designs as we need them for everything else. We're surrounded by design, but sometimes it's the old story of not seeing the forest for the trees. You have to train your eyes. We take so much for granted and are so familiar with many things that we really fail to *see* them. Next time, concentrate. Look for details you never noticed before. If you see something you like, make a rough sketch of it, or jot down something about it which will jog your memory later. You can respond as sharply to detail as you can to the whole. Use your ears, too. Often I've heard words or a phrase which brought to mind an image that might be interesting worked in a design; think of this while you're reading too, and visualize the words as you go along.

We have access to children's books for simple designs. We also have wallpaper, greeting cards, wrapping paper, magazine and newspaper ads and books of quilt patterns. We have art books too, and all of these things can evoke images which can be translated into fabric. Holidays, celebrations, family and civic life are good subjects – they've been good subjects for quilts and there is no reason why they can't be for wearables.

The "open windows" cutouts described in an earlier chapter work wonderfully well here, particularly for abstract applique. Just place the cutout over a color page or two and move it around until you like the shapes and colors which appear, then simplify the design and go on from there. Sound easy? It is.

When leafing through magazines, especially fashion magazines, I often tear out pages which appeal to me and keep them in a clipping file. It's easier than pasting pictures in a notebook, and once I'm through with them, I can toss them out.

Back in 1978, Scribners published my book *The Big Book of Applique*. It's now out of print, but it's filled with ideas and suggestions and techniques for applique. Since then, however, I've learned a lot – new ways to do things, new techniques to use, new design possibilities to explore. Applique is older than piecing; in fact, it's so old that its beginnings are lost. Maybe a prehistoric woman appliqued a piece of animal skin over a torn garment, using a sharpened piece of bone for a needle. The Old Testament tells of appliqued robes, and applique is an art easily traced back to countries all over the world. Nomads appliqued designs on their tents; the men of Africa appliqued the royal banners of Benin – and in fact, they still do; it is too fine an art to be trusted to women!

Applique can be used alone or combined with piecing, quilting, embroidery or other embellishments. All are compatible. The choice of fabrics for applique is enormous. As far as I know, there is no unsuitable fabric, so the final choice is up to you. As you know, applique means to cut a design from fabric or fabrics and sew it on top of another fabric. This is the literal definition, but again, as we all know, there are different types of applique and we'll try to get to all of them. You can sew applique by hand or machine; there isn't any right or wrong method, though the appearance or results will be different. You need not make an either-or decision, for both hand and machine techniques may be combined in the same piece. Don't feel that if you have started one way, you can't end up with another; you can. Applique, especially hand applique, is also portable. It's amazing how much you can get done in the time available to you – waiting for a train or plane, for a doctor or dentist, or for a child in school.

FABRICS FOR APPLIQUE

You can applique any fabrics or materials you can

"Myna Riot" by Sharee Dawn Roberts. Jacket has reverse applique inserts of red metallic fabric couched with metallic yarn. Photo: Glenn Hall.

"The Beast Within Me" by Sharee Dawn Roberts. Jacket and skirt of hand painted silk noil. Flower and fern appliques are Ultrasuede®, silk and polyester jacquard. Photo: Glenn Hall.

Jo Diggs' silk poncho, appliqued with flower clusters. The garment wraps from back to front and ties tightly around hips; it can be hung on a wall when not worn.

get a needle through. Whether you work by hand or machine will affect your choice; many fabrics can be used for either. Cotton fabrics, the quilt kind, are perhaps the easiest for hand applique; the poly blends tend to fray and it's more difficult to turn the edges under and keep them there. Slippery, lightweight fabrics are more easily appliqued by hand; heavier, denser and more tightly woven fabrics are more easily handled by machine. Medium weight silks are also easy to sew, as are some linens and lightweight wools, fabrics with body. Felt, Ultrasuede® and Facile® fabrics, real suede and leather do not need to have the edges turned under. Cottons come in many weights and many textures, and most of them can be used for applique. Polished cottons and chintzes are a wonderful contrast to the dull or matte finishes.

Almost all of the fabrics suitable for piecing are also suitable for applique; you can also use scraps from strip piecing or Seminole work for an applique design and add small pieces of embroidery, lace or ribbons. Large-scale prints are interesting to work with, since you get a different design every time you cut into them. Keep some checks, plaids and stripes on hand too, and anything else you think might work. If something doesn't, you can always get rid of it later. (But will you?)

TO WASH OR NOT TO WASH

Many sewers and stitchers, and certainly quiltmakers, often wash their fabrics before they take them to the sewing or quilting room. I suppose there is a good reason for this, since you don't want colors running after you've finished a project and you also wouldn't want a fabric to shrink. I wouldn't either, but I have a different approach to all this. My fabrics go directly to the sewing room when I get home. Later, when I pull them for use in garment, I decide whether or not the finished garment will be washed or dry-cleaned. Most of the clothing I make must be dry-cleaned; often, in a mix of fabrics, there are a few which can't be washed, and this decides the issue. Many fabrics which ostensibly could be washed do not wash well; they don't look as fresh or crisp afterward. The sheen often disappears from polished cotton, and washing will remove the sizing from any fabric. When you are appliqueing a design, the sizing in the fabric makes it easier to work with, so think about these things before you toss everything in the washing machine. Another thing to consider is the pressing; good pressing is as important as good sewing and if you can't press with a professional touch, don't consider washing a garment; send it to a good dry cleaners. You've spent a lot of time, energy and money creating a special wearable, so it's important to keep it looking top-notch.

THE STEPS OF APPLIQUE

Plan your applique design carefully. Decide where it will be on the garment, how much of it there will be, what type of design you will use and what fabrics will work best to highlight both the applique and garment.

I seldom sketch first, for my tendency is to cut directly into fabric. However, if I'm not quite sure what I want to do, I cut shapes from paper and lay them on the garment sections to check size, scale and position. Later I transfer the paper shapes to fabric. I also decide whether the appliques will be done by hand or machine.

Some of the fabrics you choose may be slippery and hard to handle, such as lamé, organza, thin silks or cottons. These will benefit from a lightweight iron-on interfacing. It's easier to adhere the interfacing to the fabric before cutting out the applique design, especially for machine applique, since the edges need not be turned under if you use a satin or decorative stitch or couch the edge. If you sew by hand and don't want the interfacing to extend to the seam allowance, cut the finished-size applique shape from interfacing first. *Then* apply it to the wrong side of the fabric, cut out around it, and turn the seam allowance under, over the interfacing.

Another little problem with thin fabrics is that you can see through them. Not only will the seam allowance show underneath, but the garment or ground fabric will show too, and change the color or character of the applique fabric. When this happens, back the fabric with another layer of the same fabric,

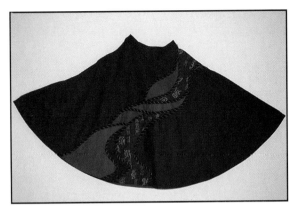

Cotton skirt in two shades of blue by Emiko Toda Loeb. Skirt sections are joined with serpentine "Fabricage" design using Celtic bias. Front view.

Back view of skirt by Emiko Toda Loeb.

if it is a solid color. If you are appliqueing with a print, back the fabric with muslin or batiste. Before you cut out shapes, put the two layers of fabric together, *draw* around the shape, then staystitch on the design line through both layers of fabric. After this, cut and sew. The line of staystitching will give you a good base for turning under a seam allowance, too.

TEMPLATES AND TIPS FOR APPLIQUE

Template material is plentiful. You can use typing or shelf paper if you need the template only once or twice; otherwise, cardboard, tag board, old manila folders or acetate can be used and all can be cut with scissors. Remember when cutting template shapes for applique, you cut to the finished size. The seam allowance, or turn under, will be added later, when you cut. Place the template on the *right* or *face* side of the fabric, and trace around it. Before you cut, think about staystitching, which I mentioned briefly a little earlier. This line of stitching, with matching thread and a fairly short stitch, acts as a stabilizer for you and is a help in hand-sewing.

Another and very decorative method, is to use a hand embroidered outline or stem stitch around the applique shape. This is a European custom and a lovely one. When you complete the embroidery, cut out the shape leaving a small turn under, then sew in place; your stitches will be completely hidden underneath the embroidery.

Freezer paper can be used for templates, too, but you must think of how you can remove it when the sewing is done. Usually, you turn the work over and cut away the ground or garment fabric behind the applique and remove the paper. You could also cut a slit in the garment fabric and ease the paper out with a pin. I have a couple of friends who stop about an inch before completing the applique stitching and pull the paper out through the little opening; this has not been a highly successful technique for me, but try it if you like.

Pressing around your seam allowances is also helpful in hand applique. Place the template over the edges of the template and press them. The resulting crease will be the sewing line you follow and this method eliminates the step of tracing around the design on the right side of the fabric.

You'll need to anchor your applique to the fabric to hold it in place for sewing and there are several ways to do this. First, you can pin. Or you can baste. You can also use a spot of glue stick, but test it out on a scrap first; sometimes it shows and you don't want that.

One of the newer and tested ways to hold an applique in shape was "invented" by the Singer research team when they were producing *The Singer Sewing Reference Library* (Random House). They used spray mounting adhesive from photography studios and it worked beautifully. The spray does not change the "hand" or character of the fabric at all, the appliques can be repositioned if necessary, and there is no residue left on the fabric. That's really a good deal; regular fabric glue spray makes it almost impossible to reposition an applique shape and it does leave a residue.

A final method of anchoring your applique is to use Stitchwitchery®, but if you do, there's no turning back, so be sure the applique is where you want it.

HAND APPLIQUE STITCHES
- *Buttonhole* or *Blanket Stitch* is a charming old-fashioned way to attach an applique. Both stitches are worked the same way, but the buttonhole stitches are very close together and the blanket stitches are separated. Such a stitch is visible, of course, so you must think of it as part of your design.
- *Running Stitch* is visible, too, and will be part of the design. Be sure the seam allowance or turn-under is wide enough for the stitches to catch; you will be sewing through three layers for this one. Take small stitches (and even ones) close to the folded edge all the way around the shape. Your thread may be matching or contrasting. If you use a silk buttonhole twist thread or embroidery floss, the effect is often very good.
- *French Knots* add a great deal of texture, no matter where they are used. Instead of whipping or blind-stitching applique, try attaching it with French knots,

BLANKET STITCH

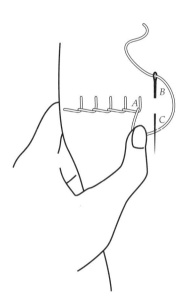

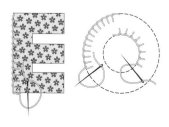

"Postcard Coat" by Faye Anderson. Jacket is silk screened dot fabric. Star constellations are embellished with buttons.

"Muñecas" by Faye Anderson. An appliqued folk art jacket embellished with muñecas, the little Guatemalan folk dolls.

using perle cotton or embroidery thread. Two or three lines of knots around the outside edge add an interesting touch, but so will a cluster of knots inside the shape or emphasizing a print in the fabric.

- *Whipping* or *Hemming Stitch*. Now we get down to business; this stitch is a small strong one. For best results, use the smallest needle you can manage, with thread to fit. A small needle will help you take small stitches. Although I have quite an assortment of needles on hand – sharps, embroidery, etc., I find I use quilting needles for almost everything. They are short and sharp, and once you are used to them, they become almost second nature. Size 9 to 10 is a good choice for any hand sewing, but use what's best for you. Bring the needle up through the base fabric, through the folded edge of the applique and as close to the edge as possible. Take the needle back down through the base fabric at the same place you first came up, then take a small stitch (⅛") underneath and bring the needle up for the second stitch. You'll have a line of little slanted stitches on the wrong side when you're finished.

- *Blind* and *Slip Stitches*. I use these stitches for my needle-turn applique and they are almost invisible. Cut out the applique shape and baste it to the base or ground fabric. The shape will be flat and you will be turning under the seam allowance with the tip of the needle as you sew. The blind stitch is perfect with this and maybe that's why they call it "blind." When you bring the needle up from the wrong side through the base fabric, it goes *into* and not *through* the fold of the turn-under, so you are sewing through two thicknesses instead of three. As in the whipping stitch, there will be a line of little slanted stitches on the wrong side.

The slip stitch is very similar, but instead of the needle going back down into the base fabric just under where it emerged, you slide the needle along the fold of the turn-under, not more than ⅛", then take it down.

Once you're used to needle-turn applique, you will probably end up preferring it. It may take a few tries to establish an easy rhythm turning under the seam allowance with the needle, but you'll get the hang of it. You could also turn the edge under with the long edge of a seam ripper. Try both ways and use the one most comfortable for you.

CUT-AND-SEW APPLIQUE

If you're working on a large and intricate applique shape, cut-and-sew may be the best technique to use.

Three of the workshops I teach in color and design for applique are Hawaiian applique, Matisse and Far Out Flowers. You all know what Hawaiian applique is. The Matisse class I call "Move Over, Matisse," and the designs or shapes are inspired by his cut-paper work done in the last years of his life. These are large, abstract shapes done with a joyous abandon and they adapt beautifully to fabric. The Far Out Flowers are so-called floral shapes – they may not look like the flowers that grow in your garden, but they work beautifully in applique. Most of these, too, are large shapes.

Instead of cutting such shapes out then basting them in place, draw the shape on your applique fabric and then cut around it, leaving a few inches as border. Position this fabric on your base or garment fabric and baste in place. When you are ready to hand applique, cut a slit along the line of the applique shape; you can start anywhere. The slit can be several inches long. Sew the applique edge in place until you come to an inch or so of the end of the slit, then cut again and continue this until you're finished. Large designs have less tendency to slip out of place or pucker as you sew, and there is less basting required for this method.

POINTS, ANGLES AND CURVES

I think people are a little scared of applique because there are a few areas which can be trouble-makers; for instance, curves, sharp points and deep angles. Once you know how to handle them, however, they can no longer strike terror to your heart.

Let's take curves first. Anytime you cut into a curve, you are cutting into the bias grain of the fabric. One of the nice things about bias is the built in stretch. If your curve is gentle and shallow, you will

Green and lavender cotton jacket by the author. Collar and front bands are heavily hand-appliqued with "far out flowers." Collection of Elisabeth Baumann.

not need to clip. As you sew, the stretch of the bias will allow the fabric to lie flat without clipping. Very deep or pronounced concave or convex curves need to be staystitched and clipped almost to the stitching line. In the concave curve, the clipping releases the fabric so that you can sew it down flat. Clipping a convex curve permits the fabric to overlap to get rid of excess and eliminates the little points or pleats which might form otherwise; it will give you a nice smooth outside curve.

An easy way to applique a circle is simply to face it. Trace the circle on the wrong side of the applique fabric. Place batiste, muslin or another lightweight fabric against the applique fabric, right sides together. Machine stitch all around the circle, then trim close to the stitching line. Make a small slit in the center of the backing or lining, turn the circle through the slit and press the seam. You now have a finished edge for a perfect circle and you can sew it in place easily with a slip stitch.

When possible, use the reverse applique technique for a circle rather than the traditional "on-top" method. Trace the circle on the *garment* fabric and cut *inside* the marked line, leaving a little turn-under. Place a piece of the circle applique fabric underneath this cut-out section, pin in place and sew the garment fabric to the applique fabric.

Another thorny little problem is sewing sharp points, but they can be handled easily when you use my "three-fold turn." An angle less than a right angle is an acute angle. When you turn under the seam allowances on the two long sides, they overlap at the point and stick out. If you cut them off, the fabric will fray. If you tuck this excess fabric in, you'll have a lumpy point. There are two approaches to a three-fold turn. First, with the tip of your needle, fold under the turn-under horizontally across the top of the point, then turn under the first long side, sew to the point and turn under the other long side and sew down it. The second approach is to turn under the seam allowance of the first long side, sew up to within a few stitches of the point, turn under the point horizontally, then complete the fold with the second long side and continue sewing. When using either

SEWING AN ACUTE-ANGLE POINT BY THREE-FOLD METHOD

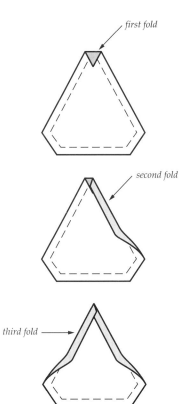

first fold

second fold

third fold

method, be sure to take a tiny stitch at the top of the point to hold it in place.

You have the opposite problem with a deep angle, for there is no seam allowance at the bottom of the V. I've read sewing instructions which tell you to clip there, but this only compounds the problem instead of solving it. It makes the V angle deeper. If it does not affect the applique design, you can roll the seam allowance under at the V angle, but then you end up with a U instead of a V. If you want to maintain the deep angle, start at the top of the V on the right side and roll under the seam allowance as you sew, but let it come to nothing at the bottom of the V. Take a tiny stitch in the V to hold any loose threads in place, then you are ready to sew the other side.

It is very difficult to start at nothing and roll a tiny hem upward, so don't try it. About an inch above the V on the left side, turn under a little seam allowance with your needle and hold it in place with the thumb and forefinger of your left hand. This will keep your fabric taut; you can continue to roll the seam allowance down to nothing at the V, then sew upward to meet your thumb and forefinger.

Some people work almost all their applique in a hoop, but I've never gotten used to doing that. However, you should work in the way most comfortable for you. Try out several ways until you find the one you like best.

MACHINE APPLIQUE

The most common way to applique by machine is to use the satin stitch. It may be narrow or wide, but should be wide enough to cover the edge of the applique completely. First, position the applique and pin in place. Now, attach the applique with either a straight stitch or a narrow open zigzag and trim excess fabric close to the line of stitching. Next, set the machine for a closed zigzag or satin stitch and try it out on a test piece first. If it looks O.K., stitch around the applique. The satin stitch should completely cover the first line of stitching and the raw edge of the fabric. When stitching, try paper under your work next to the machine bed; this will stabilize the fabric and make the stitching easier. You can tear

SEWING A DEEP ANGLE

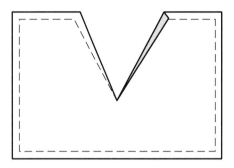

"Bog Coat Goes to a Party" by the author. Gray Facile®; machine appliqued with silks, lamé and brocade in large leaf design. Stems are couched cord. Coat edges bound with hand-dyed cotton. Back view.

Collage coat by Beryl Maddelena, showing mix of fabrics. Velvet and brocade, silks of various weaves and ribbons are sewn together and accented with gold.

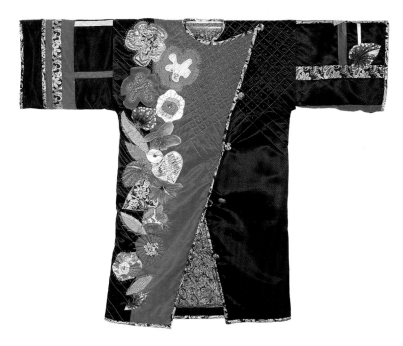

"Greene St. Garden" designed and made by the author. Black and red satin quilted with metallic thread, and appliqued with "far-out flower" designs in silk, satin, lamé, cotton and brocade. Collection of Bernice Steinbaum. Photo: Donald Waller.

"Mid-riff Lilies," the lining of "Don't Shoot the Piano Player, She's Doing the Best She Can" coat by the author. Red and purple polished cotton with appliqued lilies, broderie perse fashion.

METHODS OF COUCHING

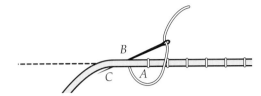

Couching a single thread or yarn with straight stitches.

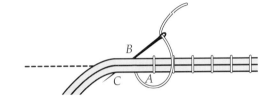

Couching two threads or strands.

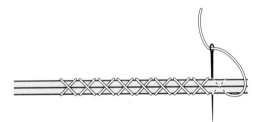

Couching two strands with cross-stitch.

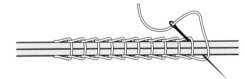

Couching with open chain stitch.

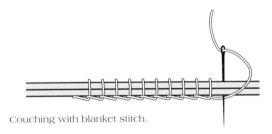

Couching with blanket stitch.

Couching with herringbone stitch.

Couching with machine zigzag.

the paper away later. Use an embroidery or applique foot on the machine instead of the regular foot; it enables you to see clearly up to the needle, as the front of either foot is open.

When your applique shapes overlap, sew the underneath one first; there is no need to stitch the part which will be concealed. The overlapping fabric will hold it all in place.

Instead of a satin stitch, use one of the decorative stitches on your machine for a change of pace, for this will also conceal the raw edge of the applique.

Machine appliqueing with a blind-hemming foot gives the appearance of hand applique. When doing this, you must cut a seam allowance and turn it under, as you would in hand applique. The blind-hemmer takes four tiny stitches in a straight line, then one zig, like half a zigzag, which swings out and catches the folded edge of the applique. If you use transparent thread in the machine, the stitches will not show at all.

DECORATIVE EDGING FOR YOUR APPLIQUES

A decorative edge around an applique shape may be just the extra touch you need to pep up the design. There are several things you can do, any of which will add a nice touch.

- Pipe the edges of your applique shape. Cut a strip of true bias ⅝" or no more than ¾" wide; fold it in half lengthwise and press. (Piping is discussed later in the Tricks and Treats chapter, too). Match edge of applique to raw edges of folded piping, right sides together, and stitch. Clip seam allowance where necessary. Press piping up; this turns seam allowance under. Position applique on garment and pin to secure. Stitch by hand, catching the piping stitching line, or stitch by machine from the top (stitching in the ditch).
- Couch the edges of the applique shape when you attach them to garment. Position the applique, then straight stitch by machine. Trim seam very close to stitching, then cover line of stitching with narrow braid, ribbon, yard or cord: couch these with open zigzag stitch in your choice of thread.
- Use an open zigzag stitch in a series of two or three

rows around the edge of the applique, one on top of another, so that stitching appears to be interlaced. Use different threads for each row of stitching.

- Another very decorative way to attach appliques is one I call Giant Zigzag. The machine stitching used is almost as important as the applique itself. I used this method on the cotton Bog Coat with floral appliques, and used it again on "Greene St. Garden" with the same floral design (Far Out Flowers). The appliques were cotton, silk, net, lamé and brocade. None of the edges were turned under. I positioned the applique shapes, used metallic thread in the machine, then simply stitched forward and backward in a giant zigzag pattern, often carrying the stitching almost to the center of the applique. I attached the leaves using "vein" stitching. This stitching is done freely and planned so it is one continuous line (see figure at right).

GIANT ZIGZAG

TYPES OF APPLIQUE

When the word "applique" is mentioned, we think immediately of the definition for traditional applique: a design cut from fabric or fabrics and applied on top of a ground or base fabric. Of course that's valid, but there are many other techniques which you should add to your vocabulary. Following are some of them.

REVERSE APPLIQUE

This is probably the next most popular and is often combined with regular applique. When using reverse, instead of cutting out a shape and sewing it on top of fabric, you cut into the fabric base following the applique shape. Place the applique fabric *underneath* the cut out space, then sew it in place. This gives a feeling of depth, for you are looking down into the applique instead of seeing it on top. Sometimes it is much easier to sew curves and intricate details with reverse applique than with on-lay applique. Fortunately you can choose either method.

STUFFED APPLIQUE

This is a three-dimensional effect and sometimes it looks a little bit like trapunto, although the technique is quite different. If you want to emphasize an

Crazy patch vest designed and made by Ardis James. The silk fabrics create a rich and elegant effect.

"Sandia Mountain Special," a jacket by Annrae Roberts. Machine contemporary crazy patchwork with recycled bell-bottomed jeans used as sleeves. Embellished with appliques, punch needle embroidery and antique buttons.

from a flower or two – and not attached to anything.

#5 is another freely cut "flower;" the lines across it could indicate Celtic bias or a couched line or reverse applique introducing another color. They could also indicate the top and bottom section might be different fabrics, joined with a plain or decorative stitching.

#6 could be appliqued flat or it could be faced and attached at the center with a button, tassel, etc. The center circle could be a yo-yo or reverse applique, or you might leave it as a finished hole revealing the ground or base fabric.

#7 Again, this is shaped from a so-called circle. It can be appliqued flat with stitching inside for texture. The inside shape could be cut separately from another fabric and appliqued; it could be treated as reverse applique, showing either another color or the ground fabric. In "Greene St. Garden," I used the reverse applique technique with a "sandwich" effect; there is a layer of silver metallic fabric covered with illusion net and between the two layers are loose sequins which move and which catch the light. Another method is to applique the large outside shape flat, face the inside shape and tack it to the other flower in the center. This creates a three-dimensional look.

#8 is the familiar tulip for applique, reverse applique or a flower having three sections (different shades). The little baby leaf #4 could be sewn in between the petals, too.

#9 Treat this flower as you would #7. The whole thing can be appliqued flat or faced and treated as a detached three-dimensional flower or as reverse applique.

Use Celtic bias for stems or cut shaped stems from fabric.

CRAZY PATCH APPLIQUE

Crazy patchwork came into vogue at the end of the nineteenth century when Victorian crazy quilts were all the rage. They were really not bona-fide quilts; they weren't used on beds and they weren't quilted. Made of velvets, silks, satins, brocades and lavish with embroidery, these "throws" were tied or tufted and lined. Every well-furnished home had at least one, folded on the back of a loveseat or draped with studied abandon on a piano. The fad gradually disappeared, but crazy patchwork stayed on.

Today you are not confined to the original fabrics; you can use anything you like – wools, cottons, linens and silk along with velvets or corduroys; anything goes. Most crazy patchwork is sewed to a foundation; you can work either in blocks or strips or cover a whole section at a time – for instance, the fronts, back and sleeves of a jacket. You can start in the middle of a section and work around it or start at the top or bottom, or in one corner. Just keep adding your fabrics until the foundation is covered, then sew them in place. The seams can be left plain or covered with embroidery or with couched cord or ribbon.

An entire garment can be made of crazy patchwork or it can be very effective used in smaller doses on collars and lapels and cuffs, for instance.

CELTIC APPLIQUE

This technique was introduced by Philomena Wiechec several years ago. Celtic design is very formal and intricate and it appears to have no beginning and no ending. Philomena developed aluminum bars to help make bias tubes for this type of applique, but I use the Celtic bias strips in a form of applique/ collage work I call "Fabricage." First, let me tell you about the bias strips, for they are an important part in the final effect.

Philomena used the bars only for marking bias strips. She stitched the fabric tubes, then inserted the bar in the tube, trimmed the seam and pressed the tube with the seam in the middle instead of on the edge. I use the aluminum bars – which come in different widths – when I sew the tubes. I fold the bias fabric around the bar and pin it in place. Then, with a zipper foot on the machine, I stitch alongside the bar, moving it downward as I sew the length of fabric. That eliminates any marking. When the sewing is finished, I trim the seam closely, then turn it so that it lies in the middle of the bias strip. I press with the bar inside, and this gives me a true bias strip ready to use. However, remember to stretch the bias as you

"Putting on the Ritz" by Judith Montano. Crazy patchwork adorns the dress bodice and collar of this lovely and elegant outfit; a matching purse completes the picture. Photo by Brad Stanton, courtesy of Fairfield Processing Corp.

Wool tweed poncho by the author. Cotton applique fabrics attached by "Fabricage" method using contrasting Celtic bias strips.

"Poppy Coat" by Jo Diggs. An elegant coat embellished with Jo's famous layered applique.

stitch; otherwise the threads may break. There is no turning involved at all with this method, since the seam is concealed beneath the bias tube when it is stitched in place. Other uses for the bias are flower stems, lattice or geometric applique, the "leading" in stained glass applique, and in weaving designs on fabric.

My "Fabricage" technique is a form of collage; you work on a foundation or base fabric, placing your garment fabrics in any kind of pattern you like; in this way it sometimes resembles crazy patchwork. This is not a stitch-and-flip technique. Once the fabrics are placed the way you want them, you are ready to sew them down – using Celtic bias. The bias covers all the raw edges of the fabrics and adds color and interest to the design. You need to study the garment section, however, to determine the sequence of sewing, since all the ends of the bias must be covered with another strip. The tweed poncho, top left, and the black corduroy jacket, opposite page, are both examples of Fabricage work, and I must tell you that the whole thing was inspired by the Dutch couture designer, Koos van den Aaker. He applies free form fabric shapes to his garments and holds them in place with bias strips of various widths and the effect is fresh and stunning, a wonderful mix of texture and color.

LAYERED APPLIQUE

Jo Diggs has developed this technique to a point of perfection in both her quilts and clothing. It gives you an easy but effective design. One of her secrets is to use a lot of fabrics so that she is able to get graduated colors in her work. Many smaller pieces, Jo feels, are better than a few big pieces. She works on a base fabric cut to shape – for instance, the yoke of a dress or the back yoke of a jacket. The design begins at the top with the first fabric layer. The second piece is laid over the first and shaped into the design line. This is then hand-sewn through the three layers, the excess fabric trimmed and the second layer pulled down in place. It is a little like strip piecing when you stitch and flip, but you are appliqueing here instead of piecing. Work your way on down the design, choosing your colors and textures carefully and trimming the excess as you go. A finished piece of layered applique is then ready to use in a garment.

WHOLE-CLOTH REVERSE APPLIQUE

This technique looks far more complicated than it is. If you wanted to use this, for instance, in a jacket (in all sections) the first things you must do are trace each pattern section and draw your design on the tracing. By working with all pattern sections at the same time you will have a unity, a flow, in your design you might not have otherwise. The next step is to choose your fabrics. Your garment fabric, for this technique, should be a many-colored patterned fabric or a solid in contrast to the applique layer. You could also piece your own yardage for a garment of this kind, but a sharp contrast is essential. Cut each garment section out of this fabric; it will be overlaid with a contrasting fabric with the design. This design is an all-over one. On the top fabric, the over-lay, trace the design carefully, cutting out each pattern piece. Match up the over-lay to the garment, section by section, two fronts, one back, etc., matching all the raw edges, and then baste in place. If you plan to hand-sew, use the cut-and-sew method described earlier. If you want to machine stitch, use a short straight stitch to outline the entire marked design, and then cut (carefully) between the stitched lines to remove the fabric and reveal the pattern. Trim these edges closely, then cover the straight stitching with a narrow satin stitch, a machine or a hand embroidery stitch or couching.

Try to simplify your applique shapes and eliminate intricate details if they are not necessary. For instance, if you are appliqueing a human or animal figure, it's easier to do it in sections if it doesn't affect the design. Add the arm and legs to the body section of a human figure instead of cutting it all in one piece. Do the same with animals; add the ears, legs and tail after the body has been sewed in place. This technique works with buildings too. Use a basic square or rectangle for the building, then add the roof or wings separately. You must weigh all of these tips and methods against your applique design and choose the ones which best serve your purpose.

A jacket by the author. Black fine-wale corduroy applied with Celtic bias in "Fabricage" technique Front view.

Back view of corduroy jacket by the author. Pants, purse and beret complete the outfit.

TO QUILT OR NOT TO QUILT:
That is the question

All garments need not be quilted. A quilted one will give you extra warmth, but aside from that, quilting adds texture, so your reason to quilt may well be an aesthetic one. If your garment has been worked on a foundation or base fabric, muslin or flannel, add a layer of batting when the outside shell is finished. The batting should be thin to keep the garment from being bulky and unwieldy and besides, you don't want to look like a stuffed pigeon when you wear it. Silk, cotton or polyester batts are all good and even a soft worn blanket or fleece will work too. I quilt many of my garments, mostly because I like the look quilting adds and I also do almost all my quilting now by machine.

There are many of you reading this who may be staunch supporters of hand quilting and that's just fine; I've quilted a number of garments in the past by hand and I may do it again some day, but I find the machine stitching easy to do and faster, and I also find the quilting design is just as effective. It's different of course; hand quilting looks like a dotted line and machine quilting is a continuous line. When you're hand quilting, you can also quilt each garment section through the lining, then join the sections together; machine quilting is much easier to do through the garment and batting with lining added later. Quilting in sections, as I mentioned, is also easier.

Each garment needs to have its own complementary quilting design and once this is decided, the choice of thread and needle comes next. This, too, depends on the design of your garment, whether it's pieced, appliqued or "whole cloth." Many designs for traditional hand quilting are easily adapted for machine quilting. Join single units together to create a long and continuous line of stitching – ropes, feather sprays and chains are examples.

I think of machine quilting in two major categories. For the first, you use a presser foot and let the machine move the fabric. For the second, you use

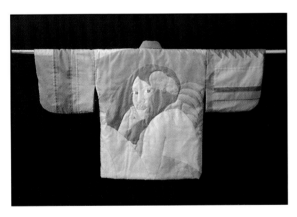

"Hawaiian Punch" by the author, back view. The silk-screened cotton print of this jacket was overlaid with silk organza, and hand quilted with one strand of six-strand embroidery floss, using the printed design as a quilting pattern.

free-motion stitching and *you* move the fabric. The presser foot works very well with straight line, grid, serpentine or gently curving lines and for outlining larger shapes.

Straight line quilting includes horizontal, vertical and diagonal lines; this includes channel and cluster quilting, grids (diamond or other), plaids or checks. When quilting from side to side or top to bottom, there's no worry about the starting and ending threads for they are all caught eventually in a seam. When I quilt "randomly" I stitch without a pattern in mind, creating and crossing lines in several directions. Use a presser foot, too, for outlining large shapes and perhaps even filling in some details. All of this type of quilting with the presser foot can be done with either a single or double needle; remember to try a test piece first when choosing pattern, thread, needle or needles.

Presser-foot patterns usually need to be marked. Try chalk or soap slivers; both can be brushed off later and will not damage your fabric, although you'll have to mark at the last minute since the marking won't be visible indefinitely. Masking tape can also be used to mark straight lines for most fabrics. Lay a strip of tape ¼" *away* from the stitching line, so that you don't mash the tape into the fabric as you stitch. The presser foot will ride alongside the tape. When the stitching is finished, gently peel off the tape and place it for the next line. You should be able to use the tape five or six times before discarding; don't leave the tape on the fabric indefinitely.

Early in this chapter I mentioned you would be machine quilting through the garment and batting alone and adding lining later. This is the technique I use most of the time, but it is also possible to quilt through the lining, if that is the effect you want. It is a little more time consuming to start and stop – unless you stitch to the edge – since the threads need to be tied off separately, but again, if you've planned a "long line" of quilting, you won't have to contend with this very often. Also, if a quilted lining is important to you, you could quilt both the garment and the lining separately then put the two sections together. It is also possible to quilt the lining without quilting the gar-

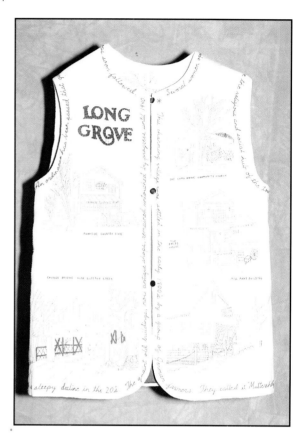

ABOVE: Front view of "Thread Sketches" by Shirley Fomby. Free motion machine stitched "drawings" also serve as a quilting pattern. BELOW: Back view.

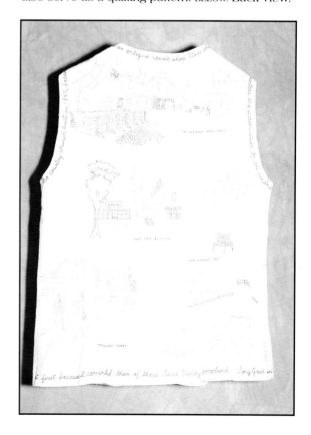

ABOVE: "There's a Hot Time in the Old Town Tonight" coat open to show lining, quilted in sections with diagonal grid and double needle and two colors of thread. INSET: coat lining.

Wedding outfit by Rita Zerull; dress with long sleeveless quilted satin coat embellished with needle lace. Photo by Brad Stanton, courtesy Fairfield-Concord Fashion Show. See detail page 102.

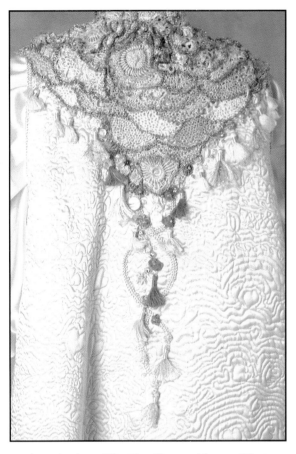

A close look at Rita Zerull's machine quilting on the satin coat shown on page 101. Rita calls this "doodle" quilting. Note the stunning needle-lace collar, and the hearts in the quilting design. This is free-motion work.

ment; there may be enough pattern and color in the piecing or applique of the garment shell that it needs no addition.

The coat of my outfit "There's a Hot Time in the Old Town Tonight," is of black polished cotton, unquilted, but the lining was quilted in panels with a diagonal grid and two-needle stitching, then added to the coat.

Free-motion quilting does not need to be marked unless you are following a definite design. This type of stitching is done with the feed dogs dropped or covered and a darning foot replacing the regular presser foot. Since you and not the machine are moving the fabric, it is easy to create any type of design as tiny or intricate as you like – doodles, hearts, flowers or even words. Set the machine at half speed if you can and move the fabric slowly while pressing the foot pedal at full speed. Keep both hands on the work to create pressure and keep the fabric taut. "Meander" and "stipple" quilting are both done this way and even a little of this on a plain surface will create a wonderful design with added texture. Sashiko designs also can be done with machine stitching, but you need to chart your direction ahead of time. Using free-motion, you can also bead-quilt – adding a seed bead to regular stitching at planned intervals.

The wonderful selection of threads we have available today has elevated both hand and machine quilting in garments. In addition to regular sewing thread, there are metallics and rayons which can be threaded through the needle assembly; both of these add glitter and shine to your work. Several years ago special thread had to be wound on the bobbin, so that you were quilting from the wrong side of the garment, but that isn't true today of the ones I've mentioned. Whenever you choose any sewing thread, choose the thread first, then the needle to fit; when working with metallic thread especially, use a needle a size larger to eliminate friction in stitching. Double needle stitching with these threads also creates a stunning effect.

Other "special" threads still must be wound on the bobbin – perle cotton, yarns, crochet cottons and mini-ribbons. This means, of course, that you will be stitching from the wrong side of the garment. Silk buttonhole twist is another thread which must be used in the bobbin and each of these will add a lot of texture and interest to your quilting.

Whenever you quilt, the garment section should feed evenly through the machine. If you have a problem there, try the even-feed or walking foot attachment. Using paper underneath the work, next to the machine bed, will stabilize the work for you too, and this is especially helpful with double needle stitching. The two needles are controlled with one bobbin, which makes a zigzag stitch on the wrong side. Without the paper, this stitch sometimes has a tendency to pull up to create a ridge, so keep that in mind.

Zigzag stitching used for quilting is also a possibility for interesting patterns. Used closed, as with satin stitching, it creates a bold definite line; use it open and it gives a more lacy appearance. I quilted a vest several years ago with a satin stitch, but used it in what I called a jack-straw pattern. The satin stitched lines were only two or three inches long and crossed each other like jack-straws; there were four in each cluster, three of bright different colors and one of metallic. A graduated satin stitch is effective too; start at nothing and graduate the stitch to its widest point, then bring it back to nothing again.

Couched quilting can also be done by machine. Mini-ribbon, either ⅟₁₆" or ⅛" wide, rat-tail cord or yarns all work well. Hold them in place with a zigzag, using either matching or contrasting threads and following a design of your choice.

TRAPUNTO QUILTING BY MACHINE

Trapunto consists of a combination of Italian cording and stuffing, and both are worked through two layers of fabric. Usually a thin fabric such as batiste or other thin cotton, even muslin, is fine. You can mark your trapunto pattern on the backing fabric, baste it in place, then stitch from the wrong side and no marks at all will be visible from the right side of the garment. Use a straight, short machine stitch, with either matching or contrasting thread. Cording

"Innocence" by Shirley Fomby. Silk leaves are hand-quilted through ½ thickness of batt, and edges left raw. Shirley's inspiration for the jacket is from Genesis 3:7: "...so they sewed together fig leaves and made coverings for themselves."

patterns are stitched in channels about ⅛" wide, then the channel is filled with yarn or cord, which gives it a raised appearance. When the stitching is completed, use a size 16 or 18 tapestry needle to thread the channels. Work the yarn with your fingers as you go along, so that it lies flat against the fabric.

Stuffed trapunto needs only one line of stitching, rather than the two needed for cording. With two layers of fabric together, stitch around the design completely. You can draw the design on the backing and stitch from the wrong side, but you can also use many of the printed fabrics of today for stuffed trapunto work. Choose the section you want to stuff, then place the backing fabric behind it and stitch from the printed fabric side, around the design. Turn the work over, make a small slit in the center of the backing fabric and stuff through this slit, using small bits of polyfill. Don't stuff too tightly; a little goes a long way. When you're finished, close the slit. Trapunto designs can fill the body of a garment or be used as accents on collar, cuffs and belt.

Designs for machine quilting are as varied as they are for hand quilting, and you'll think of many which can give your work a very special look. If you want an all-quilted garment, you can quilt yardage ahead of time, then lay the pattern sections on the fabric and cut and sew. If you want a *real* short cut, you can purchase pre-quilted fabric and save yourself a lot of time. I do this occasionally, but I also add to the quilting to make it more interesting. I spoke earlier of Sashiko quilting and how effective some of those designs are. Sashiko is really planned for hand stitching and as you probably know, is a form of stitching traditionally done with a soft white cotton thread and used to hold two layers of cloth together in Japanese garments. It not only strengthens, but also decorates the garment; the designs are traditional Japanese symbolic and ritual designs and are stitched in a continuous line. There are several books and magazines which have instructions for this, but I think one of the best books is *Sashiko Quilting* by Kimo Ota. You can order it from her at 10300 61st Ave. S, Seattle, WA 98178.

TYING A GARMENT

Tying is an alternative to quilting for your wonderful wearables. It also adds texture and design. When I was growing up, we had a lot of tied comforters for bedding. They really looked like quilts, except they were tied and not quilted; tying is just another way of holding all the layers in place so they won't shift. You can tie with yarns or perle cotton, using double knots or adding little yarn pompoms. You can also tie with buttons, beads, tassels and French knots or add bits of ribbons and tiny strips of fabric. Tying is done by hand rather than machine, and it also takes much less time than hand quilting.

I hope none of you will misunderstand my bypassing hand quilting in this chapter. In no way am I trying to belittle it; hand quilting is still an accepted and marvelous way to stitch a garment. However, I think most of you are already very familiar and perhaps experienced in it and might have very definite ideas of what you would like to do when you create a special garment. Machine quilting is not new, but it's new to many people and it is only in the past few years that quilters and sewers alike have been experimenting with it and finding out how wonderfully versatile it is. It is a relatively new field, with increasing acceptance, and it offers tremendous possibility for you to add to your quilting vocabulary.

My book *Quilts To Wear*, originally published by Scribners and now reissued by Dover, deals entirely with quilted garments, both hand and machine, and this could give you added information on quilting wearables.

TRICKS AND TREATS:
Fabric manipulation, fabric embellishment and surface design

Those of us whose lives are consumed and governed by fabric and its possibilities probably grew up learning to cherish it and handle it with loving care. We were careful not to snag it, stretch it out of shape, tear it or otherwise abuse it. "Playing" with fabric, exploring it and experimenting with it, however, is an exciting invitation to changing its character and personality. Artists are constantly changing techniques and approaches to create new effects, and we can do that too – in fact, we already do. We pull, twist and wrinkle; we stitch in decorative instead of functional ways; we quilt with puckers and gathers; we stretch and stuff fabric; we combine fabrics in unheard-of ways; we change the direction of pleats; we ignore the grain, and we've come up with a whole new bag of tricks and treats – ones definitely not injurious to our health. In fact, these tricks and treats may even relieve stress.

These tricks and treats are ones I use in my workshops and my own clothes. None of them is really new or original; they have been used in one form or another throughout fashion history. Today, in both garments and accessories, these same techniques can be revived and changed and added to our work. They are as adaptable for modern clothing as they were for clothing a hundred years ago or more. They add both interest and texture, as well as color accents, and we can pick and choose as to their placement and frequency of use. The challenge is constant. The variations are endless.

PLEATS AND TUCKS

Pleats and tucks are members of the same family, and they have a great deal in common. Tucks are usually stitched down their full length; they are ornamental and add interest and texture to fabric. Pleats are functional and also decorative. They are used to control and release fullness in certain areas of a garment, but other times they may have no function at all except to be eye-catching.

Both pleats and tucks have a long history. They have played an important part in both men's and women's fashions throughout the centuries. Pleated ruffs, pleated flounces and pleated sleeves were as common as pleated skirts or shirts or dresses. Long before flat irons came into being, Egyptians used hot stones to "press" pleats into fabric. Perhaps you've seen some "crisping irons" in a museum display; these antique tools set the pleats in some of the elaborate trims so popular from time to time. Today, we mark and baste our pleats, then press. We can also use pleating boards, and if we are really serious and have a lot of meticulous pleating to do, we can send the fabric off to a pleating company which does nothing but pleat fabric on a commercial basis. Occasionally, if we're lucky enough to find it, pleated fabric is offered for sale in some shops.

There's a neat little invention out now to help you with pleating. It's called "The Perfect Pleater." It is about eleven inches long and contains a series of louvers set ¼" apart. Thus you can have quarter-inch pleats, or skip every other louver and have half-inch pleats. You can also pleat in clusters. The fabric is tucked down into the louver, so it should not be too heavy; a medium to light weight works well. A thin ruler helps to push it snugly into place, and you can also use a credit card.

When the pleats are formed, press with the fabric still in the Perfect Pleater. Dip a press cloth in a solution of white vinegar and water for permanent pleats. Be sure to let the pleated fabric dry thoroughly on the pleater before removing. Other suggestions and tips are included in the instructions for the Pleater. You may find it in shops, or it can be ordered by mail from Clotilde, Inc., 1909 S. W. 1st Ave., Ft. Lauderdale, Florida, 33315-2100.

Pleats may be stitched part way down, or not at all. There are box pleats, inverted pleats, knife and accordion or sunburst pleats. Box and inverted pleats are the reverse of each other; a box pleat on the outside of a garment becomes an inverted pleat on the inside – and vice versa. Knife pleats go in one direction and are of uniform size. They are pressed to one side, and may or may not be stitched down part way. Accordion or sunburst pleats are pressed only; they are used most often on circular skirts, capes or collars, and they start from nothing and increase to the desired size at the bottom or lower edge. They fan out, or flare, and because these pleats bellow out when the garment is worn, they are fittingly called "accordion" pleats after the musical instrument.

There are three basic types of tucks. Spaced tucks, as their name suggests, have a space between each tuck. The space may be any width, and may be even or uneven. The second type is blind tucks, which usually overlap each other. The third, and most popular, is pin-tucks, those wonderful little decorative touches which add so much to a garment's detail. They are raised and should never be pressed flat. They are usually about a sixteenth of an inch, and can be spaced or clustered. All types of tucks are formed on the outside of a garment, whereas pleats can be formed either from the outside or inside. Both pleats and tucks can be hand or machine sewn. Both need to be marked and stitched accurately for best results.

In the past few years, many sewers and quilters have created interesting effects with fabric by using blind or spaced tucks and pleats, and turning them in the opposite direction at intervals to form a design; the pleats or tucks are held in place with either a decorative hand embroidery stitch or a line of machine stitching which forms a design line.

Pleats and tucks both have tremendous decorative possibilities. They flatter when used in the shoulder and neck area. They add fullness and interest in sleeves as inverted or knife pleats which originate at the shoulder seam. These sleeves can be fitted below the elbow to form a long cuff, or they can fall free into a bell-shaped sleeve. Balenciaga, the great Spanish designer, used pleats to dramatize cape-like sleeves in a simple shaped scarf coat. He formed the pleats in horizontal rows, using narrow taffeta ribbon inside as a stay. The pleats created an interesting and unusual effect. Mario Fortuny, the great Italian designer, was famous for his finely pleated silk garments around the turn of the century. He called these Delphos; made of beautiful silks, chiffons and satins, they were simple, columnar forms with tiny, unstitched permanent pleats from top to bottom. Unfortunately, Fortuny died without passing on his secret, although many designers and home sewers have accomplished wonders in their own pursuit of pleating.

Both pleats and tucks need to be marked accurately, then basted and pressed, and all of this takes time. The final results will be worth the time, however, if the pleating is essential to the style of the garment. It will be easier to work on a flat surface, basting as you go.

FAKE FORTUNY

Many years ago in Italy, Mario Fortuny added to his list of accomplishments a method of very fine and rather irregular pleating using lightweight silks. Made into simple column-like gowns, the pleats were permanent, and as I mentioned before, the secret of making them died with Fortuny. Since then many people have tried to achieve the same type of pleating, and some of them have come very close or succeeded very well. Such pleating has become a trademark for Mary McFadden, and others less known have become equally successful, using both silk and polyester fabric.

I've tried it, with natural fabrics, and as a form of fabric manipulation it adds a great deal of interest to

"FAKE FORTUNY" PLEATS

"Fake Fortuny" pleats used as inserts with commerical patterns for a unique look.

both garments and accessories. The first method I developed is one I call "Fake Fortuny," and instructions for it follow. The second method is detailed under "Wet and Wrinkled," later on in this chapter (page 125).

INSTRUCTIONS: Use light to medium weight natural fabrics, such as cotton, silk, linen or sheer wool. Use a sheet of typing or shelf paper as a stabilizer, and pin the paper to a piece of foam core. Cut a strip of fabric the width you want and several times longer than the finished length you need. Pin the top of the fabric to the top of the paper. Use your fingers to make tiny pleats (don't try to measure), pinning each side as you work to hold the folds in place. Keep them as close together as possible, and work horizontally to the bottom of the paper. Now lift the fabric and paper off the foam core with pins still in place, and slide one edge of it under the presser foot of your machine. Stitch the length, removing the pins as you go, then repeat for the other side. Keep the paper in place and press. This pleated fabric can be used as patches or strips, joined by seaming or it can be used as applique shapes, geometric, floral or abstract. Cut a paper template the size of the patchwork or applique. For instance, if you want to use a 3" x 7" strip in a pieced garment, cut paper 3" x 7", lay it over a section of the pleated fabric and pin it in place. Now machine stitch around the paper template; this holds all the pleats in place, and afterward you can remove the typing or foundation paper, for the stitching will hold the pleats for you. Follow the same method if you want to applique. Use paper templates, pin in place, and stitch around them, then cut them out. I did this for several big leaves of the floral appliques for "Bog Coat Goes to a Party," using lamé and other glitter fabrics. These tiny pleats can be left as is, or they can be turned to go in the opposite direction, and held in place with a bead or a French knot. The turning creates movement in the fabric. If the pleated piece is wide enough, the pleats can be turned two or three times, alternating direction, and instead of beads or French knots, you can hold them in place with machine stitching.

These tiny Fake Fortuny pleats rely on stitching to

hold them in place, although the pleats themselves are not stitched down unless they are turned. Most other pleats are also left free, although some are stitched part-way; a pleated skirt could be stitched from the waist to the hip area and the fullness of the pleats then released. In contrast, tucks are almost always stitched their entire length; that really constitutes the difference between pleats and tucks.

Tucks may be any width, depending on where they will be used. It takes care and time and patience to mark them, but once they are stitched you can use them as you would any plain fabric. One of the wool quilts in the Denver Art Museum's collection is an antique beauty, made entirely of hexagons, each of which consists of ¼" tucks. The hexagons are joined so that the tucks constantly change direction, and the effect is fascinating.

Once tucks are stitched, they can be used in any direction in your work – horizontally, vertically or diagonally. Tucks can also radiate from a central point; they can fan out, crisscross each other and appear at almost any angle. Tucks used with striped or plaid or checked fabric take on an added dimension, and pin-tucks are especially effective.

PIN-TUCKS

These tiny tucks are only about ¹⁄₁₆" wide and until fairly recently, most were hand-sewn. Exquisite infants' dresses and slips, as well as ladies' blouses were often hand-pin-tucked in sheer batiste or lawn. Machine tucking, of course, is faster, and now some of the newer computerized machines have special feet which will tuck in clusters of three, five, or seven etc., and this is a great time saver. If you don't have one of these feet and are stitching one tuck at a time, fold the fabric then stitch very close to the folded edge – this is almost like edge-stitching, except that you will repeat the process for as many tucks as you need. You can simulate pin-tucking in some fabrics by using double-needle stitching. Since the needles are governed with one bobbin, the stitched line pulls up or "ridges" a little, and looks like a pin tuck. When you want the stitching flat, use paper underneath to stabilize it.

Whenever you plan to use either pleating or tucking as inserts and accents for a wearable, pleat or tuck the fabric first, then cut. This tucked fabric could be used in strip piecing, or, for that matter, any other type of piecing or applique work. When you're tucking fabric, try different effects. Cluster the tucks; stitch tucks into plaids or checks or grids. Pin-tuck a section of fabric, then cut it up and sew it back together so that the tucks now lie in a different direction.

Tuck a transparent fabric and use it as an overlay, then tuck fabric with a cluster of pin-tucks, then a cluster of ¼" tucks, then back to pin-tucks. Use bright colored yarn to thread the larger tucks in sheer fabric and create a new effect.

PUFF PLEATING

Remember those biscuit or puff "quilts" of a few years back? They really weren't quilts; they were big puffy covers looking to all the world like overstuffed biscuits crowded together. They were made into bed covers, into purses and tote bags and muffs and, so help me, into vests! Like the novelty it was, it died early – but the memory lingers on.

The biscuits were made of two squares of fabric. One square, the smaller one, was the foundation. The top square was cut larger, usually by an inch, sometimes by an inch and a half or even two inches. The top half was placed over the bottom square, and the excess fabric pinned out in a pleat on each side. With raw edges matching, you stitched around three sides, stuffed the biscuit with polyfill through the opening, then completed the stitching.

This fad didn't last long – the fate of most fads – and while cleaning out some boxes some years ago, I found samples of the biscuit. These were unstuffed, strips of biscuit-work ready to be completed, and they were also mashed pretty flat from being packed away. The look of the strip fascinated me, and got me started in what I now call "puff pleating." I tried out different sizes of squares, then branched out into diamonds, circles, hexagons and triangles and began to add this new fabric manipulation to my work. I really thought (for awhile) I had invented something new, until I saw a silk quilt made in 1890. The entire top was composed of unstuffed biscuits!

PENCIL PLEATS

These are also called "cartridge" pleats, but I call them pencil pleats since I use a pencil to form them. Use either a crisp fabric with the edges finished or turned under, or a fairly heavy grosgrain or satin ribbon. Strips of pencil pleats can be inserted between two pieces of fabric, or they can be stitched directly to foundation fabric – the pocket or sleeve of a jacket, for instance. They must always be worked on a foundation. If you want to insert them between two pieces of garment fabric, use a foundation compatible to the garment fabric, for it will show a little bit. The pleating strip, either fabric or ribbon, should be the finished width you want to insert; the foundation strip should be wide enough to include seam allowances.

Center the pleating strip to the foundation strip at the top and stitch across to hold in place. Now slip a pencil in between these two strips and fit it snugly against the stitched line. With a zipper foot on the machine, stitch alongside the pencil, starting and stopping at the edges of the pleating fabric. Repeat this process until there are enough pleats for what you have in mind. Such a strip can be inserted in a purely decorative way; it could also border a Chanel-type jacket.

These pleats, when used on a sleeve at the shoulder, or on a pocket, can be formed directly on the garment fabric before the sections are all sewed together. Center the pleating strip at the shoulder edge of the sleeve and stitch it in place. Form the pleats as outlined before and stitch to hold. Usually five or six pleats at the sleeve top are enough. If you use the pleats on a pocket, continue the pleats for the entire length of the pocket. If your fabric or ribbon is crisp, these pleats will stand up like little soldiers, and they should, for best effect.

Choice of fabric always makes a difference in the appearance of any type of fabric manipulation. Often, a solid color shows up better. This is true of puff pleating, and it is also true of "off-set pleating," another idea you may like to try. There is no hard-

and-fast rule about fabrics used in "Tricks and Treats." You may be happily surprised with some unlikely choices.

SINGLE PLEATED STRIP, OFFSET

Offset pleating is also done in strips, on a foundation fabric, and I call it "strip-pleating" since that term happens to describe it pretty well. Strip-pleating changes the texture of any fabric used; it creates an area of interest. Strips are formed with either single or box pleats, but the pleats are off-set, staggered, a clear contradiction to the idea that pleats must be precise and even!

• Cut a foundation strip the desired width. This may be muslin, flannel, or your garment fabric. Try 2" or 2½" for starters.

• Cut a fabric strip for pleating ¼" wider than the foundation strip.

• Lay the pleating strip over the foundation and stitch together at the top.

• Work on a flat surface. Working with your fingers, form a small (½") pleat along one side at the top; pin in place. Pleats can go either up or down, but be consistent.

• Form a pleat on the opposite side, but not parallel to the first. For a ½" pleat, the second pleat formed should start about ½" below the one on the opposite side.

• Continue in this manner. The off-set pleats will form a soft V down the center of the strip, and the extra ¼" width is taken up with this. As you work, the edges of the pleating and foundation strips will be aligned.

BOX-PLEATED STRIP, OFFSET

• Cut a foundation strip the width of the pleats.

• Cut a strip for pleating ¼" wider than the foundation.

• Lay pleating strip on top of the foundation strip and stitch or pin the two together.

• Starting at the top, form a box pleat on the upper right side of the strip; pin. Work from side to side, so the next pleat is on the left side of the strip, but drop it half the width of the pleat. When you've made a few in this manner, it looks like one side is box-pleated and the other side is inverted-pleated. Continue until the strip is filled, then machine stitch along each side to hold the pleats in place.

RUFFLES AND FLOURISHES

Ruffles come in all sizes and fabrics, and are as popular today as they were a couple of hundred years ago. They have a soft, feminine look to them; they are flattering when used around a neckline, framing the face. They can be used around the edges of sleeves, or the entire sleeve can be made up of layered ruffles. Ruffles form jabots, they take the place of peplums, and they can also be used as inserts in seams or around the hemline of a skirt. They can be pleated or gathered, flat or circular.

FLAT RUFFLES

Flat ruffles are cut on the grain of the fabric – lengthwise, crosswise, or bias, and they can be single or double. They should be cut on a ratio of 2 to 1 at least; that is, to insure proper fullness, cut the ruffle twice as long as the area it is to cover. If the fabric is thin and sheer, you should cut it 2½ or 3 to 1. It is easier to finish the edge of a single ruffle before it is gathered or pleated, and you can do this either by hand or machine. Hand-rolling takes a lot of time, but it is an elegant finish. The narrow-hemmer attachment of your machine will give you a nice finish too; another possibility is zigzagging the edge, or serging it – if you have a serger. A double ruffle, of course, needs no hemming. Fold the fabric lengthwise in the middle, press it, then gather the two layers at the raw edges as if they were one. Bias-cut ruffles are much easier to handle if they are cut double instead of single, and because of the grain, they fall or drape beautifully.

CIRCULAR RUFFLES

The distance from the small circle in the center to the outside edge is the width of the ruffle plus seam allowances. Slash the circle from the outside edge to the small circle on the straight of the grain. Seam slashed edge of one circle to slash in another and continue until the ruffle is long enough. These ruffles

CIRCULAR RUFFLES

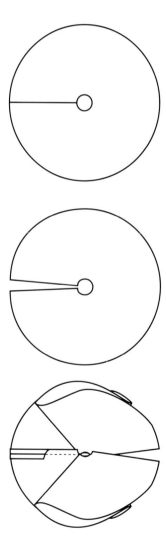

The distance from the small circle in the center to the outside edge is the width of the ruffle plus seam allowances. Slash circle from outside edge to small circle on straight of grain. Seam slashed edge of one circle to slash in another and continue until ruffle is long enough. These ruffles made of circles stitched together in a continuous line are very full.

made of circles stitched together in a continuous line are very full.

We usually think of ruffles as gathered or pleated on one edge only, but you can make an interesting ruffle trim by finishing both edges of the fabric strip then running the gathering stitches down the middle. This is a technique you can use on a soft ribbon too.

Circular ruffles are the frothiest ruffles of all. The radius of the circle is the width of the ruffle, plus ¼" seam allowance. Cut each circle from the outside edge to the center, on straight of grain, then cut a tiny circle (½") from the center for seam allowance. When you have cut several circles for ruffles, stitch the slashed edge of one to the slashed edge of another and so on until the ruffle is long enough. If you are working on a single ruffle, use French seams on the joins. If the ruffle is double, a narrow seam at the joins is sufficient, but you will need twice as many circles for a double ruffle. Place right sides together, stitch along the outside edge, trim the seam, turn and press.

Circular ruffles are similar to flounces, since both are stitched on without gathers. The circular cut does the ruffling for you.

RUCHING

Ruching is another form of gathering, but both long edges are gathered instead of one. A ruched strip can be inserted in seams to add decoration or color or change of texture, and the result is very effective. Since both sides of the ruching strip are gathered, it's quite easy to go around curves; you pull up the gathers on the inside curve and let them out on the other. A ruching strip may be stabilized by using a foundation strip of thin, woven material, although some ruching strips may be applied directly to a garment section.

SOME TIPS ON GATHERING:
• Lengthen the stitch on the machine to 3 or 4. Stitch the full length of the ruffle on the seam line, then stitch a second line immediately above the first, in the seam allowance. Pull on the two bobbin threads simultaneously and distribute the gathers evenly.

- A second method is to zigzag over a thin cord, then pull on the cord for gathers. Be careful not to catch the cord in the stitching.
- Try the gathering foot or the ruffler attachment of your machine.
- Use elastic thread in the bobbin. Stitch, holding fabric taut. When fabric is released, gathers form.

Ruffles and flounces were commonly used throughout different periods of fashion history. A look at the fashion magazines of today will convince you they are still popular in one form or another, changed to meet the needs of modern times, and modified or enlarged to suit individual taste.

SMOCKED GATHERING.

Smocking has been a popular needlecraft for many years; it is still very much in vogue, especially for infants' and children's dresses. It is also used on blouses; it not only adds a stretch feature, but often one of design too. There are a number of books out filled with directions on different types of smocking; there are also stamped patterns available. Smocking is too limited in scope for me to give it space in this book, except for one technique worthy of mention. It is a simple but effective way of smocking, an aberration really, devised by Rita Zerull. She calls it "chained" gathering because she uses the chain stitch to draw up the fabric. The finished effect is one of smocking. It is best done on thin material. Rita gathers her rows about a half-inch apart. She starts by taking five or six small running stitches through the fabric on the gathering line, pulls up the stitches and secures them with a chain stitch. She continues in this fashion throughout the succeeding rows. Her thread is perle cotton, which is not only strong enough to hold the gathers without strain, but is also decorative.

RANDOM SMOCKING

Remember that smocking goes a lot further than little girls' dresses. Smocking is a form of gathering. After the gathers are formed, they are caught with stitching to hold them in place. All this, of course, is a form of fabric manipulation, and you don't really have

"Tricks and Treats" cotton jacket by the author. *Turned tubes* make the closure; *puff pleating* is the pocket. *Turned pleating* is on the collar. Sleeves have piped seams and *off-set single and box-pleated strips*, and are embellished with yo-yos and faced circle flowers.

Back view "Tricks and Treats" jacket. Top back V yoke is *wet and wrinkled*; bottom center is *Fake Fortuny* pleats with beads. *Prairie points* and scallops are used as *seam inserts*. Sections are separated with *Celtic bias* strips. Notice seam inserts throughout jacket.

to follow any set of rules to do your own smocking, and you don't need to transfer a set of dots to guide your stitches. For instance, you could run five or six rows of gathers about ¼" apart, in parallel rows, either vertically or horizontally, along the fabric. Do this either by hand or machine, then pull up on the threads until the gathers are as full as you want them to be. They don't have to be even, in fact, often they look more interesting if they aren't. When the gathers are arranged to your liking, stitch over the gathering threads either by hand or machine. Use a chain, outline or feather stitch by hand, and any decorative stitch by machine.

TUBES: VARIATIONS ON A THEME

Usually, a tube is round, but a fabric tube may be either flat or stuffed, depending on how you want to use it. A tube, joined with its fellows, can also be woven, braided, knotted, turned, stitched and tasseled. It may be cut on either the bias or the straight grain, can be any width, or color, and works better with a light to medium weight fabric. Tubes have myriad uses, either functional or decorative, and will give your wonderful wearable a special look.

SPAGHETTI TUBES

These are mini-tubes, made with bias strips of fabric and filled with heavy string or butchers' cord. They were used as straps on flapper dresses in the twenties and thirties – and even now are used this way: sometimes one tube, sometimes two or three. Spaghetti tubes are also used to make frogs for closures, as decorative designs on garments (held down by couching), or as fabric fringe and tassels. The tubes are similar to purchased rat-tail cord, but they have the advantage of being made of the fabric of your choice. They can be used to fasten collars or neck-pieces, as shoulder straps for a purse, to decorate a belt, or as ties for lacing, faggoting and closures. You may well find other uses for them.

There are several types of tube turners on the market, and some of them are pretty good. I find it easier, however, to use string for turning spaghetti tubes, perhaps because I'm used to it.

These tubes must be made with the true bias of fabric. Cut a strip about one inch or 1¼ inches. Although these are tiny, narrow tubes, you want the folded fabric wide enough so that it won't slip out from under the presser foot.

Fold the strip in half lengthwise, right sides together. Now cut a length of string or butchers' cord TWICE as long as the strip. Find the mid-point of the string and stitch it firmly across the end of the fabric strip on the right side of the fabric. Stitch back and forth a few times, so that the string will not pull out. One-half the length of the string will be folded inside the bias strip, and the other half will be free. With a zipper foot on the machine, stitch snugly next to the cord or string, along its length, but be careful not to catch the string. Use a short stitch, and stretch the bias as you sew; this will keep the stitches from breaking when you've finished.

There should be an inch or less of cord extending from the stitched tube; trim the seam, then pull on this cord. Since the mid-point of the cord was stitched to the other end of the fabric, pulling the cord will start the tube to turn, and when it is all the way through, it will still be filled with half the length of cord while half of it hangs free.

You started with a cord twice as long as the bias strip; the upper half after turning is now inside the tube and you can decide whether or not to leave it there. Remember that bias stretches; if you plan to use the tube where stretch is unwanted, leave the cord inside. Also, the tube will hold its shape better with the cord.

FLAT TUBES

For a one-seam tube, cut a strip of fabric twice the desired width plus two ¼" seam allowances. These tubes can measure from a half-inch to two or three inches, depending on the use you have in mind. Fold the strip lengthwise, right sides together, and stitch one-fourth inch from the raw edges, then turn and press the seam. The seam can lie along one side, or, if you plan to stitch both sides of the tube later, move the seam so that it lies in the middle. When the tube is stitched, the seam will be completely concealed.

Jacket by Mary Lu Stark. Tubes or strips of jewel colors are woven into stunning design for the front and back of this cotton jacket. Edges of tubes are finished by serger and tacked in place with buttons.

gathering the fabric the length of the collar. I stitched through the cords at each end of the collar, cut the cords, then bound the collar edges. Long stuffed tubes (½" wide) are used as ties; they are attached in an ornamental way to each end of the collar, and the whole corded collar is stitched to the body of the cape.

So far, in TRICKS AND TREATS we've changed fabric from two-dimensions to three, and in a fairly traditional way – with pleats and tucks, ruffles, and flat and stuffed tubes. Any and all of these techniques change the appearance of fabric and in doing so, change the texture too. There are a number of other ways we can manipulate fabric and change its character and appearance, and some of them are strong contradictions to our early learning.

Remember, how as you were growing up, you were taught to take care of your clothes? Don't cut or slash or tear; press carefully, get rid of wrinkles. Don't snag or tear a hole in your garment, and take precautions against shrinking them unintentionally. Don't use hot water with wool and silk; remember that fabrics, especially natural fabrics, are living fibers. So we were taught.

Yet when we dive back into fashion history, we find one particular form of fabric mutilation popping up time and again – that of slashing the outer layer to show what's underneath.

Henry VIII was noted for his slashed clothes. He was a vain man who loved to dress elaborately and expensively, but it was his tailor who came up with the idea of slashing Henry's outer garments so his fine silk underwear would show. He got the idea, strangely enough, from the battlefield. Seeing uniforms ripped and torn, he transferred the idea of slashes to court clothes and started a new fad. Henry was delighted; he wanted the sumptuous fabrics of his court clothes to be noticed by all, and if they were slashed, the finery underneath would be glimpsed too. He had slashes on his sleeves, his chest, and on his breeches. Both fabric and leather were treated in this fashion.

Slashing fabric was popular in Germany as early as the sixteenth century. Often an entire garment was slashed to form a design or a series of designs. The Three Musketeers wore slashed leather jackets; the backs were especially heavily slashed. Spain adopted the fad and used the slashing technique to create flower petal designs. In France, Marie Antoinette was so impressed with the needlework on her petticoats that she had her dresses slashed in the front to show the embroidery underneath.

Back in England, ladies' fashions kept pace with the men's. Often, the slashed fabric was caught with buttons or jewels. Sleeve fashions for both men and women advocated huge turned back cuffs with slashed undersleeves showing.

Many of Queen Elizabeth's costumes were also slashed, and of special note was her favorite riding habit. The habit itself was heavily trimmed with leather and quilted with cord. The sleeves of the habit were leather too, ornately quilted, embroidered, then slashed at intervals to show color underneath.

In the present couture world, Zandra Rhodes of England uses slashing in her clothes. And a number of years ago, here in America, Tim Harding introduced the technique in his unique line of clothing. He has raised slashing to an art form, and his garments are explosions of color and design. Tim uses simple jacket and coat shapes, some based on the Japanese hippari. Most of his garments are cottons hand dyed in brilliant colors, then layered, stitched, slashed and otherwise mutilated and then washed. The washing frays the slashed edges of the fabric and creates even more texture. As the edges are fluffed up, the layers separate a little and the color variations are dazzling. Tim used geometric designs for many years, but recently he has developed a line of "landscape" coats with intricate and varying colors. His work is not only body art, it is wall art. A few years ago, Tim's slashed designs sparked a flurry of imitations in the quilting world, and "blooming" vests and jackets and tops became popular for awhile, then gradually faded from sight.

In the mass market, Georges Marciano slashed the jeans in his GUESS line of clothing; many of them look as though the fabric had caught on a nail.

"Cloak of Night" by Tim Harding. A simple functional shape for this layered cotton coat assures maximum opportunity for interlacing and smocked design. Photo: Stanbitz/Thiesen.

"Aspen" by Tim Harding, a cotton great coat reflecting Tim's training as an artist. This is part of his landscape series. In his work, he changes and molds old techniques into contemporary forms. Photo: Petronella Yisma.

SLASHING

Slashing is not confined to overall design. Rita Zerull of California uses the technique to embellish clothing with "cut and slash" fabric flowers. These shapes are circles of varying sizes, made up of stacked layers of fabric. Rita stitches first through all layers about ¼" from the outer edge, then she stitches another circle closer in. She then slashes between the stitched lines, being careful not to cut the bottom layer. Sometimes she also slashes an X inside the inner circle. She uses the same technique on squares and hearts, and often the stitching is a close, very narrow zigzag instead of a straight stitch.

FABRIC FRINGE

There are several ways to create fabric fringe. The obvious one is familiar to most of us; you choose a rather loosely woven fabric and pull out the weft threads to the desired length. You might use a short fringe, say about an inch long, to finish the sleeves and hem the edge of a jacket, and use it also on the bottom edge of a skirt. Scarves, of course, are regularly finished in this manner.

A separate fringed Chanel-type braid can be easily made from strips of fairly loosely woven fabric. Cut a strip about two inches wide, then fringe both sides of the strip to a depth of a half-inch. Next, fold the strip lengthwise so that one-fourth inch fabric shows above the fringe, and top stitch by machine close to the fold. This fringed braid makes a very decorative trim, especially when made of the garment fabric. It can be attached with a second row of stitching along the folded strip, placed below the first stitching and just above the start of the fringe.

You can make very interesting fringe on many fabrics simply by slashing with scissors; this is more effective when the fringe is longer – perhaps six or seven inches, or even more. Don't try to measure these cuts as you make them, just cut very narrow strips. They probably won't be straight, but that won't detract from the overall effect so don't worry about it. You could even add a few beads now and then to the fringe, or tie some of it in knots to create more texture.

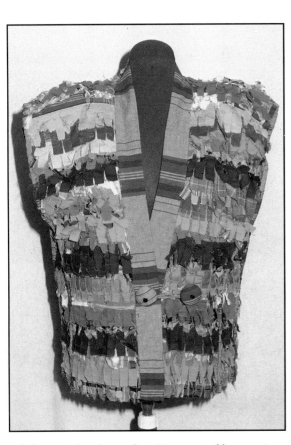

"Rich Rags" by the author. Vest cut of heavy gray cotton; "rags" are folded strips of fabric torn into fringe, layered and stitched in rows.

Experiment with several different types of fabrics, for the fringe will look different on each of them.

FURROWED FABRICS: WET AND WRINKLED

Sounds like you're plowing a field, doesn't it? It may be similar, after all, for you can "plow" furrows into your fabric to create some fascinating effects. This is part of the Fake Fortuny pleating I told you about earlier, except that the fabric looks to be more wrinkled than pleated.

Use a natural fabric – cotton, silk or linen – and wet it. Squeeze out the excess water, then twist the fabric into a tight rope, pulling it to form tight close wrinkles. Let it dry this way; it may take a few days. If you're in a hurry, slip the fabric into an old pair of panty hose and toss it in the dryer. When it's dry, untwist it, keeping the wrinkles intact, and pin the fabric to a foundation. I used this technique for the back of my "Tricks and Treats" jacket, in a triangle yoke form; Lucy Poffinbarger used it as long panels in her sleeveless panel coat (page 127).

Stitch the wrinkles in place on the foundation fabric, follow the lines or creases in the fabric and stitch only as far as each wrinkle or furrow goes. This means you'll be breaking stitching often, but it's more effective this way, and you can change colors of the thread too. Don't backtack; pull the threads through to the wrong side and tie them off. Lucy used tiny red floss inserts when stitching, and beaded the entire section by machine. I used free-form inserts, small shapes faced with contrasting fabric, then stitched into a pleat so the raw edges wouldn't show.

You can also insert slivers of fabric, ribbon or yarn, or leave the stitching as the sole decoration. When I was growing up, we pleated summer cotton skirts in a similar fashion; while wet, we slipped a pole inside – usually a broomstick –, pulled the wet fabric down tightly against it and tied it in several places. Our "pleats", however, were not stitched down at all, but hung free without any pressing.

"Wet and wrinkled" designs vary. Instead of pulling the fabric vertically into a rope, wad it up, squeeze it, and tie it loosely in a knot. This manipulated fabric, once it is stitched and ready to use, can be included

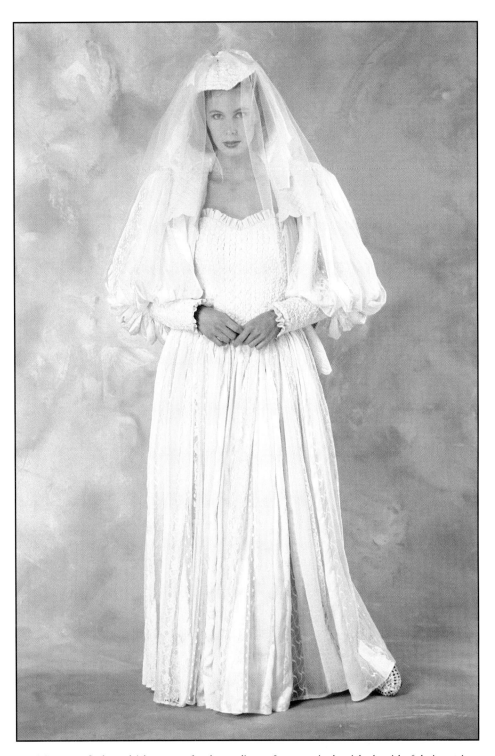

Wedding outfit by Shirley Botsford. Bodice of gown is braided with fabric strips which release fullness into skirt. Photo: Brad Stanton, courtesy Fairfield Processing Corp.

TOP LEFT: Long vest by Lucy Poffinbarger. Body of vest is gray cotton, "wet and wrinkled." "Wrinkles" are machine stitched with various color threads and beaded throughout; seam inserts are tiny tufts of red floss. Textured fabric is combined with bright floral print. Collection of Deb Casteel.

TOP RIGHT: Back view of Lucy's vest.

RIGHT: A detail of beaded stitching in Lucy's vest.

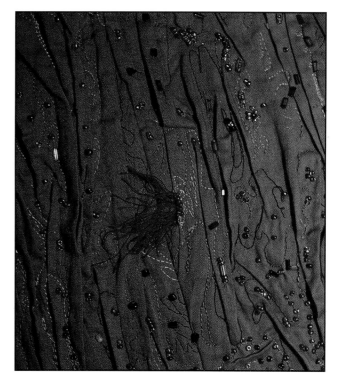

in a garment, or an accessory. You'll see some of it in belts and other accessories as well as jackets.

Cut the pattern piece from foundation fabric, and place the wrinkled fabric on top of it, pinning the corners so that all the base is covered. Now you're ready to stitch, and this should be done by machine. You can use vertical serpentine stitching lines fairly close together to hold all the wrinkles in place, but I think it is much more effective to stitch the wrinkles vertically. They'll be broken, so your stitching will be too; this means a lot of starting and stopping, but as you stitch, pull the threads through to the wrong side and tie them off before they get all tangled up. Change the color of thread as you go along, if you like, or keep it all the same. The wrinkles, or some of them, will form little lop-sided pleats. You can insert slivers of fabric, ribbon, yarn or floss under some of the wrinkles if you like, and you can punctuate your stitching with beads, as Lucy did.

You can get different wrinkled designs by handling your wet fabric differently. Instead of pulling it into a rope to create a fine broken vertical pleat, wad it up in your hands, squeeze tightly, then put it down gently and let it dry. Or you can tie some loose knots in the wet fabric, and end up with still another set of wrinkles, which can be stitched in a different pattern. I've used small patches of this in some of the belts I've made, and as you study the photos, you can see the nice contrast of texture.

SEAM INSERTS

Decorative seams can add as much design to your wonderful wearable as patchwork, applique or other embellishments. Seams, whether construction or otherwise, can be emphasized in many ways, and using seam inserts is one of the most effective. Piping, both corded and uncorded, prairie points, scallops, free-form shapes, ribbons, laces and ruffles are all part of this and can add a great deal of interest and color to a garment. You might make a sampler for yourself and keep it handy for reference; use left over fabric strips and use as many different seam inserts as you can think of.

PIPING

I stumbled on flat or uncorded piping some years ago. I had been using corded piping for a long time, and making my own with butcher twine. One day, out of twine and in a hurry, I used the piping flat and have been doing it ever since. Piping usually is quite narrow; uncorded piping can range from ⅛" to ¼". There isn't any law which says it can't be wider, and the garment itself could help make up your mind. For ⅛" piping, cut strips ¾" wide, fold them lengthwise, and press. These strips can be either straight or bias grain, depending on what you're sewing. As you well know, if there are curves, the piping must be bias. A straight grain piping stitches easily into a straight seam. This piping strip, folded, includes two seam allowances of ¼" each, with ⅛" fabric showing. To insure a straight seam, match the raw edges of the piping strip to the raw edge of one garment seam, and machine baste close to but not quite on the ¼" seam line. Now place the other garment section on the one just stitched, right sides together with the piping enclosed. Turn this sandwich over so that the first line of stitching shows; it is your guide, and you can stitch right next to it without having to measure.

Flat or uncorded piping strips may be layered also, but you'll have to trim some of the seams afterward to reduce the bulk. Piping strips would be ¾", 1", and 1¼", folded and pressed, then stacked with raw edges meeting. Machine basting along this stacked edge will hold everything in place until you're ready to sew. You can also stack corded piping, but they will be heavier in bulk and look; try a sample before you start the real thing.

Piping is an accent for your garment, so choose the fabric carefully, not only for color but also for texture and pattern. Bias piping with checks, stripes and plaids is always effective; lamé piping adds a touch of glitter and shine to everything. Remember to stretch bias as you sew, and pin the raw edges together so they won't slip. If you need a lot of bias, use the full width of your fabric with the crosswise and lengthwise grains at right angles to each other. The long folded edge created is the true bias, and I prefer this method to the "continuous" bias method;

PRAIRIE POINTS

1st METHOD   2nd METHOD

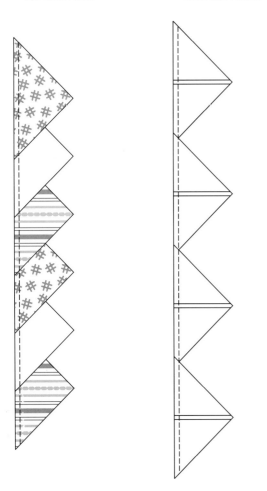

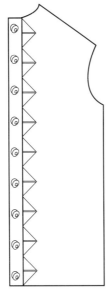

Front of garment showing Prairie Points made with Method #2 stitched in the front band.

there are far too many seams in the latter and I think they detract from the overall effect.

SEAM INSERTS

Prairie points are another very popular seam insert. They have been around for years, used on quilts as well as clothing. Some antique quilts were bordered with prairie points, either in one or two layers; they were also used in seams in the interior of the quilt, but all of these trims have also been – and are – used in garments. This edging has been described variously as Dog-Tooth, or Van-Dyke edging, but we know these points as prairie points

There are two "official" ways of making them, and I have added a third, my own "fake" version. For all methods, cut a square of fabric; this will vary, depending on the finished size, and you might want to try out some samples in paper before you cut a lot of fabric squares. Start with a 3" square, and go up or down from it.

For the first method, fold the square on the diagonal, then fold it a second time on the diagonal. You now have one closed folded side of a triangle, and a folded open side. The closed side of one triangle will slip inside the folded open side of another; how far inside, is up to you.

In the second method, the fabric square is folded horizontally; mark the midpoint of the folded edge, and bring each side down to the raw edge at right angles. This leaves the folded opening in the center of the triangle rather than at the side, as in the first type.

In the version I added, Jinny's fake prairie points are really faced triangles. Place two fabric squares together, right sides facing, and stitch all the way around them. Cut the square diagonally to make two triangles. Trim the excess fabric from the corner, turn and press.

These are effectively used in any kind of piecing; you could use them singly, in twos and threes inserted in the seams, or filling the seam line completely. You can also stack them, using a smaller one on top of a larger, but remember this may cause a bulkier seam and you'll need to do some trimming or feathering later.

A prairie point "stacked strip" is a three-dimensional eyecatcher. Use it as a substitute for a regular strip in a random strip-pieced garment; you'll love the results. Use the second method of making them with the opening in the center.

You'll need a base or foundation strip for this, either garment fabric or muslin; cut it wider than the prairie point. Start at the bottom with a prairie point centered on the strip, the point down and the folded opening visible. Stitch the prairie point ¼" from the raw edge at the top, through the base fabric. Now add a second prairie point over the first, so that the bottom section of the first will be visible. Stitch the second prairie point in place and continue in this manner until the base strip is covered. You're ready then to incorporate it in garment piecing. The strip is complete as it is, but if you want to add further details, you can tack down the points with a tiny bead or an embroidery stitch.

Folded ribbons, instead of fabrics, can also be used for prairie points, and don't forget that varied textures will add interest too, such as silk prairie points used on cotton, or gold or silver lamé used against a plainer background. Couture designer Pierre Cardin once made a whole sculptural dress covered entirely with prairie points. You could do that too, so don't be afraid to experiment.

SCALLOPS AND OTHER INSERTS

Scallops are circle tricks, and the technique is the same as in my "fake prairie points," except that one uses a triangle and the other a half circle. For scallops, cut circles of fabric in whatever size you choose. Place two together, right sides facing, and stitch all the way around. Now fold the circle in half and cut along the fold, then turn and press. Each circle makes two faced half-circle scallops. Use them the same way you use prairie points

GEOMETRIC INSERTS: RECTANGLES

Folded strips of fabric with the ends tucked in can be used for seam inserts too. These should be short, of various widths from ⅛" up to ½", and inserted at random in the seam as color accents. Overlap or

GEOMETRIC INSERTS: RECTANGLES

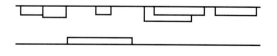

FREE-FORM FACED INSERTS

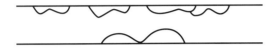

"Get Me to the Church on Time" by the author. Dress of three white fabrics from Concord House, from Marinda Stewart's T dress pattern. Made for "Cut from the Same Cloth" invitational challenge coordinated by Marinda Stewart. Dress also incorporates safety pins, hooks and eyes, ribbons, elastic and many other notions, all part of the challenge.

stack them too.

FREE-FORM FACED INSERTS

Make these from scraps. Put right sides together then stitch randomly to create a free-form insertion. After stitching, trim seam closely, turn and press.

Although I've been telling you about fabric inserts, don't forget there are many others: bits of ribbon, especially the mini-ribbons, bits of yarn, lace, or narrow fringe.

TEXTURAL TREATS

This chapter is about changing the appearance of or adding to your fabric to create three dimensional and textural interest. We've already explored a number of techniques, but here are a couple of other simple ones you might like to use someday.

NICKEL AND DIMING IT

On the wrong side of your fabric (light to medium weight silk, cotton or wool) draw around nickels or dimes so that the circles are fairly close together. (You could use quarters too, of course.) Choose a thread to match or blend with your fabric, then hand sew around each circle, pulling it up into gathers, then secure the thread and go on to the next. You'll be working from the wrong side, but these circles will become a nest of gathered puffs on the right side ready for use in a wearable or accessory.

LET'S MAKE WAVES

This is a form of gathering, and may be done either by hand or machine. Draw wavy lines on the wrong side of your fabric, fairly close together, then stitch on the lines and draw the threads to gather.

DESIGN STITCHING

Add interest and texture to your fabric with machine stitching. Use a variety of threads, and double as well as single needles. Stitch geometric shapes, stitch a plaid or checked design, or stitch at random to break up the surface of the fabric. Stitch between the wales of corduroy or pique, and add stitching to a printed fabric.

FABRIC EMBELLISHMENTS

Yo-yos, those funny little gathered circles, are not all dead-end. I remember the yo-yo coverlets of years ago – I thought they were dreadful. Little gathered circles were tacked together in some form of design, then spread on top of a colored sheet and used as as bedspread. These were real toe-catchers! There were also yo-yo dolls and clowns at church bazaars and I couldn't see any long distance virtue in yo-yos at all until ten or so years ago. It occurred to me then that you could transform them into yo-yo flowers and use them as you would other fabric flowers – so I did. In a variety of fabrics and sizes. Adding beads and buttons and ribbons, you can transform their lifestyle.

You do remember how to make them, don't you? Cut a circle, or cut several circles, different sizes. Fold under a tiny bit of the raw edge and by hand, do a running stitch all along the outside edge. Pull the thread up into a tight gather, and fasten off. Attach them through the center and use a button or bead to cover the tacking stitches.

Yo-yos may also be attached around the edges with beads or French knots, or even whipped securely in place. Add a tiny bit of polyfill for a stuffed look, or sew on ribbon or rat-tail streamers. You can also use a shi-sha mirror in the center, but it will have to be glued in place inside and the yo-yo gathered around the mirror edge.

OTHER CIRCLE TRICKS

Half circles will also make fabric bells or cones. Use contrasting fabrics; you'll need two half circles for each cone. Fold the half-circle so that the raw edges meet, and stitch the straight side in a ¼" seam. Do the same to the second half-circle. Now put them together, right sides facing, and stitch around the curved edge. Cut across the point of the cone (not much, just a little) and turn the cone through this hole. Press seams. Fold under the raw edge at the point of the cone and tack the cone or bell in place on your fabric, covering the point with buttons or beads. You can also slip ribbons or cords into the

"When Yo-Yos Last in the Dooryard Bloomed" by the author. Yoke is heavily machine quilted in black and embellished with yo-yos, circle flowers and spaghetti tubing. Celtic bias in checked fabric outlines yoke.

"Now I Lei Me Down to Sleep" by the author. Hand batiked and hand quilted muslin coat, embellished with yo-yos.

Opera coat by Annrae Roberts. Velvet coat lined with glitter and adorned with three-dimensional flowers.

PREPARING STRIPS FOR MAKING FABRIC FLOWERS

trim

cone and out the slit at the top, and let them hang free. Another way to cover the point is to attach it with a tiny yo-yo.

Those faced scallops you made from circles can also be transformed. Layer them on a base fabric, starting from the bottom, then cover them with a second layer so that they are overlapped. They look a little like clamshells but they'll give you a great three-dimensional effect.

Another way to use them is in flowers and leaves. The scallops can be petals of a flower, and to be most effective, you should use two or three sizes, with the smallest in the center. As you work your way around the flower, take a little pleat in the straight side of the scallops, and tack them all in place. For variety in your "floral arrangements," cut the basic shape as an oval instead of a circle and proceed as before. It will give you a different look.

FABRIC FLOWERS
REBEL ROSES

No time to make a quilt? Use your fabric scraps and strips and make a nosegay instead; use a fabric flower corsage on a belt or a bag; use separate flowers to embellish a choker necklace; cover a collar or a little jacket with flowers, or the bodice of a dress, and be the belle of the ball.

You can use ribbon or fabric strips for the flowers; the width and length of the strips determine the size. Use any medium to lightweight fabrics – sheer fabrics in silks and cotton are especially pretty.

Cut fabric strips either on the straight or bias grain, wide enough to fold in the middle lengthwise. After folding, the strip should be at least 2" wide for flowers; anything narrower could be used for buds. The length will vary. Use at least 12" to 14", and cut some strips the full width of the fabric for larger flowers. Try both straight and bias cuts.

Fold the strip in half lengthwise and pin the cut edges together. If this fold is unpressed it gives a soft look to the flower, and is best if used with soft drapey fabrics. You may also stitch an open zigzag along the fold (keep fold lined up with center of foot). Use a contrasting or metallic thread for this. If you want to shape your flower specifically, zigzag over a fine wire.

Stitch a gathering line through the raw edges of the folded strip, starting at the fold at one end and curving down to the straight edge. Trim excess fabric.

Pull up the gathering thread and roll the strip up with your fingers to form a flower. Tack through the bottom to hold everything in place, and cover raw edges with ribbon or fabric if necessary.

A Bedouin wedding dress, heavily embroidered.

A Saudi-Arabian dress embroidered with gold in a mosque design.

EMBROIDERY:
When more is better

All the "Tricks and Treats" in the last chapter are, literally, little tricks you can do to change the look or character of your fabric, add to it, or subtract from it. One of the age old ways to add to fabric is with embroidery. Up until fairly recently it was always hand-embroidery. Even though we've had machines for a long time, the embroidery skills are fairly recent in machine stitching. Each machine has its own personality, so each of you will have to develop your own rapport with your machine as far as embroidery is concerned. There are some excellent books out on the subject, and even your instruction book – the one which came with the machine – can get you started. It probably includes basic instruction for embroidery, and if it doesn't, look under *darning*. Put the darning foot on your machine, drop or cover the feed dogs, loosen the top tension, then practice. The instructions no doubt tell you to use a hoop to keep the fabric taut, and this is excellent advice, at least while you're learning. Later, use your hands instead of the hoop to get tension on your fabric. The free-motion aspect of this type of stitching enables you to go in any direction. Changes in tension, both upper and lower, give you varied effects, as do using a variety of threads, many of them wound on the bobbin. If you plan to use your machine for free motion embroidery, treat yourself to an extra bobbin case and keep it just for embroidery. If you play around with the tension of your machine, and you have just the original bobbin case, it is sometimes difficult to reset it correctly when you want to do plain sewing again.

You can get a lot of embroidered effects with the zigzag stitch in different lengths, different widths, and with different threads. Remember to choose the thread first, then a needle to fit. If you have a machine with built-in embroidery or decorative stitches, by all means use them. Test the stitches out first. Try them with a variety of threads, use them alone or in groups or in combination. You may have surprises at home you didn't know about.

Many good needlework books and magazines are filled with elaborate embroidery and suggestions for using it. Hand and machine embroidery may be used separately, or combined. Certain types of embroidery are identified with cultures from all over the world; South and Central America emphasize different embroidery and applique designs, and often this work serves as a means of identifying a village, a society, or an individual. The history of embroidery is long and fascinating, but there is space here only to help you with a few basic stitches, the cornerstones of design. Use embroidery to enhance a solid color, and use it on prints to emphasize and accent the design already there. Embroidery added to your wonderful wearable, whether a little or a lot, can truly make your garment special.

BASIC HAND EMBROIDERY

Embroidery has always been with us – thank goodness! What a plain, unembellished life we would lead without the beauty, the elegance, and the excitement of the threaded needle and its possibilities for color and design. In some instances, embroidery has been compared to painting; it not only graces walls, but covers our floors and our bodies in many different ways. It adds surface design and embellishment to fabrics, and, happily, we can get some wonderful effects with only a limited vocabulary of stitches – the very basics. And here they are.

You may know these already, but for those of you who don't, if you think of them as families or groups of stitches, it is easier to understand them. Remember that the size of needle will change the appearance of a stitch, and so will the thread or floss or yarn you use. The color, the texture and the weight all contribute to appearance, so that the possibility for design is endless. If you master six or seven basic stitches, you will then be able to combine any of them to create different designs which will look complicated and complex – and aren't at all. That can be your secret.

FLAT STITCHES

Four flat stitches are the basics. The running stitch, the satin, outline or stem, and herringbone are

Modern day caftan from the Arabian peninsula.

FLAT & CHAIN STITCHES

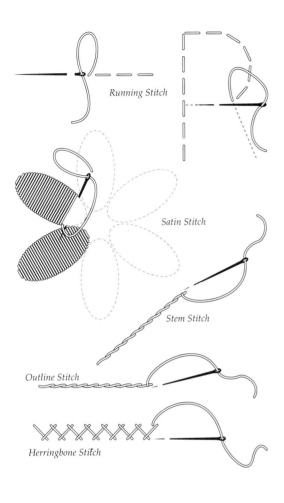

Running Stitch

Satin Stitch

Stem Stitch

Outline Stitch

Herringbone Stitch

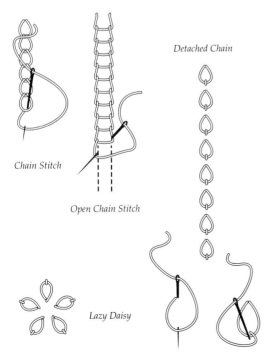

Detached Chain

Chain Stitch

Open Chain Stitch

Lazy Daisy

the four. Running stitches are really a series of straight stitches. Sew from right to left. The stitching will appear as a broken or dotted line, and you can use it for outline or filling. You can also applique with it. Straight stitches used in a circle can be flower petals, or, slanted, they become rain. You can "thread" a series of running stitches by weaving another thread or yarn in and out of the line.

When straight stitches are laid next to each other to create a solid surface, you have a satin stitch. The word "satin stitch" makes us think of machine stitching immediately, because satin stitch has become such a staple in our sewing and such a common and easy way to applique or create texture. It is also possible to do satin stitching by hand. In fact, the hand stitching was popular long before sewing machines were invented.

Outline or stem stitches are also in the "flat stitch" family; there is only a small difference between the two. While working the stitch, if the thread is above and to the left of the needle, it is an *outline* stitch. When worked in the opposite manner, with the thread *below* and to the right of the needle, it becomes the *stem* stitch. You work both of them from left to right, and the stitch gives a solid, instead of broken, line. A convex curve is easier to do with the thread above, and the concave curve is easier to handle with thread below.

The herringbone stitch is the last stitch in the "flat stitch" family. It is also worked from left to right between two imaginary parallel lines, either straight or curved. In this manner, you can use it to join seams or bound edges. It can be used as insertion too. It is a flexible stitch, with an open or closed look depending on how close together the stitches are. You can also vary the width and follow any direction the design dictates. You can use this stitch for hemming too, but then its name changes to "catch stitch," since its purpose is to catch two layers of fabric together.

CHAIN STITCHES

As you can see from the diagram to the left, this is a vertical stitch, again worked between two imaginary lines, for an open chain, and on one vertical line for a single closed chain. Separate chain stitches can also be worked in a circle to create a flower – as in the lazy daisy stitch. A detached chain stitch is often used for leaves.

LOOPED STITCHES

This family of stitches includes buttonhole or blanket, feather stitch, fly and Cretan stitches, and turkey work. Buttonhole and blanket stitches are really the same, except for spacing. The buttonhole stitches are very close together, as you know; blanket stitches are not. The direction in working is left to right, and it is a horizontal stitch, worked between imaginary parallel lines with the outside line the finished edge of a garment – or blanket or quilt.

A feather stitch is worked almost like a blanket stitch, except that the direction is vertical instead of horizontal, and the stitches alternate from right to left along a single vertical line. The fly stitch is a variation of the feather stitch, and sometimes is called a "Y" stitch because it looks like one. It is really a single feather stitch, with the thread loop held in place with a tacking stitch, but it can be used in a series as well as singly.

The Cretan stitch is similar to the feather stitch, and usually worked vertically, although you can work it horizontally and also around in a circle. It has great possibilities for texture, and is one of the stitches we use to attach shi-sha mirrors; the other is the buttonhole stitch. The Cretan stitch is worked alternately, from side to side, and a spine is formed between the two sides. This spine *can* be in the middle, giving an even, regulated look to the stitch, or it can be off to one side with the stitches forming spokes. It is easy to master, but you must remember to keep the thread below the needle so that a loop is formed.

Turkey work, or tufted stitch, is also part of the looped family of stitches. The stitches form loops above the surface of the fabric, and worked close together, they look like tufting. You don't knot the thread for this one, but leave the end of it free on the surface of the fabric above the first stitch, as in the diagram.

LOOPED STITCHES

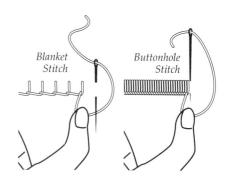

Blanket Stitch *Buttonhole Stitch*

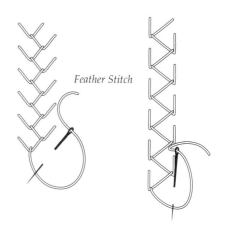

Feather Stitch

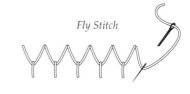

Fly Stitch

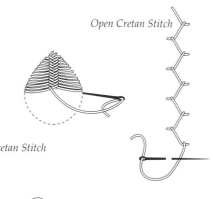

Open Cretan Stitch

Cretan Stitch

Turkey Work Stitch

ABOVE: "Diamonds Are a Girl's Best Friend," silk jacket by the author. Heavy black silk is quilted to Cotton Classic® batt in grid pattern with gold thread to form diamonds. Lapels and insets are plaid Thai silk, hand embroidered with metallic thread and flosses, shi-sha mirrors and couched cords. BELOW: Back view of the jacket.

When you start, if you're having trouble holding the mirror in place, put a spot of glue on the back to anchor it, then follow the diagram. One set of foundation stitches probably is sufficient to hold it in place, although often I do two of them just to be on the safe side. When the foundation network is complete, you simply use an embroidery stitch, either a buttonhole or a Cretan, and stitch through the foundation into the fabric all around the edge of the mica. This conceals the foundation stitching completely, and adds ornamentation. I'm sure there are other embroidery stitches you could use, but the Cretan and buttonhole are the most common and they serve the purpose very well. You can work the buttonhole stitch either way, with the finished ridge inside and the spokes outside, or the other way around. You can also vary the Cretan stitch so that the spokes are uniform or irregular, and then, if you can't let well enough alone, extend this embroidery with rows of stitches, French knots, or beads for added sparkle. Shi-shas are both washable and dry-cleanable, so no need to worry. I once saw some shi-shas attached with a lazy daisy stitch, and the effect was petal like, and more open than the other.

Earlier, I mentioned that Aardvark Adventures also carried plastic rings to fit the shi-shas. These are little white plastic things that fit over the mirrors; first, you cover the ring completely with buttonhole stitches so that none of the plastic shows, then do your additional stitching through the fabric and the stitches covering the ring. This is a fast and easy way to attach them too, and the effect is somewhat different. Try them both!

TASSELS AND TRIMS

Tassels are a romantic and elegant trim and they alone can change an ordinary garment or accessory into a special one. They have long been used in the home furnishings field as well as the apparel field. You can buy tassels in almost any shape or size and have your choice of yarns or fibers; you can use them as is or add a few embellishments of your own. Good tassels, however, are expensive, and if you need more than one or two, you might consider making them.

The basic tassel is very simple. Decide what type yarn or floss to use, and how fat or full you want the tassel. Cut a 3" wide piece of cardboard the length of the tassel, and lay a piece of yarn across the top of the cardboard for tying. Now, with the tassel yarn, wind around the cardboard and over the tying yarn until the tassel is as full as you want it to be. Various yarns, threads and ribbons may be added to the winding too. Tie one end securely with the yarn length you've been winding over, then cut through the loops at the bottom end of the tassel and remove from the cardboard. The next step is to wrap the neck of the tassel. Use the same yarn if you like, or change to a metallic or anything else that catches your eye. Hold the tassel yarns together below the tie and wrap securely over the loose end you started with. Wrap tightly down ½" to 1", depending on the size of the tassel. Then thread a large-eye needle with the wrapping yarn, and take a stitch underneath the wrapping up through the center of the tassel and out the top.

Basically, that's about all there is to it – except that you can really accentuate the positive when you're dealing with tassels. First, you can cover or decorate the head of it with a detached buttonhole stitch, which gives a nice little cap-like effect. Add yarn or other beads to the neck of the tassel and insert some here and there in the tassel itself. You can also build up on the neck of the tassel with wrapped cords, rings or spools to make it as elaborate as you want.

BASIC TASSEL

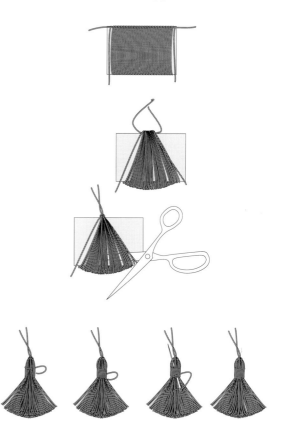

ACCESSORIES:
Extra added attractions

Accessories are the last word, the final touch, and they are essential – the right ones, I mean. When you've made a very special wonderful wearable, the rest of the outfit must be absolutely right for it or the magic is lost. You don't want to overwhelm your new wearable, but you certainly need to accentuate the positive. Take time to choose the right jewelry, the right bag, the right shoes and gloves and if you are as smart as I think you are, you will have been thinking about them since you started the garment; maybe you already have the right things on hand!

There are other times, however, when you can use accessories in the opposite way. Instead of underplaying them as complementary to your garment, you can use important accessories to change a very plain outfit into something very striking. The very plain outfit serves as a foil for the accessory, and this is something to keep in mind when you don't have time to make a garment. Spend time on a bag, a belt, a neckpiece/collar or hat to add that extra pizzazz. Depending on what you make, your accessories can change the plain outfit into an elegant one, a sporty one, or one somewhere in between. Good accessories are expensive, it takes time to shop, and even then you might not find the perfect accent so pull out your scraps and let your imagination fly! You can make fabric jewelry, bags, belts, neck pieces and body ornaments and while you're at it, it might be a good idea to make some for Christmas or other gifts. And had you thought about the perfect solution for travel? When you want to travel light, take two or three basic plain pieces, and some accessories – including scarves. By following this suggestion, you can get everything you need in one bag and have a change of costume for every event!

SCARVES AND SHAWLS

Scarves are indispensible and I'm sure you have quite a collection. – everybody does, square ones, long ones, pleated ones, in prints and plain, silk and chiffon and other fabrics. There are dozens of different ways to wear or tie a scarf, and there's even a book listing one hundred of them, complete with diagrams, and that could keep you busy for a long time!

Shawls are somewhat different; in the first place, they are bigger, and in some instances they can easily serve as wraps on a mild evening. These are easy to make – and you can make gorgeous ones for a fraction of what they would cost ready-made – if you could find them. Wool challis, or other thin wool, is wonderful fabric for a shawl. It's lightweight, and it's wide, usually 54". If you buy a yard and a half, you'll have a large square. Now, roll the hem, or use fringe around the edges, and it's done. Silk usually is only 45" wide, so a square shawl of silk would be smaller – unless you add borders. The border should be a double one, so cut it twice as wide as you need, and long enough to miter the corners. Stitch the right side of the border to the right side of the scarf, and miter each corner as you come to it. Since this is a double border, the miters will be in opposite directions, so you stitch the miter from the corner of the scarf to the center of the folded border, then change direction and stitch the miter on the lining side of the border. It's easier to do this as you come to them, rather than trying to plan ahead.

A scarf may be square or rectangular, and even the six-foot scarves are popular. Hem the ends, or add fringe. Most square scarves are folded in half diagonally when worn, so they look like triangles, but you can also make a triangle scarf. When the triangle becomes oversized, it is called a shawl. This can be a single layer of fabric, or it can be faced. Scarves and shawls can be pieced or appliquéd or embellished, as you would any wonderful wearable, and they can easily become an important part of your wardrobe.

BODY ORNAMENTS OR OVERLAYS

Overlays take many shapes and forms and can be worn over plain tops and skirts, or tops or turtlenecks and pants, over a plain dress, or even over a coat or cape. There are photos of several styles for you to look at and get some ideas. I made the diamond

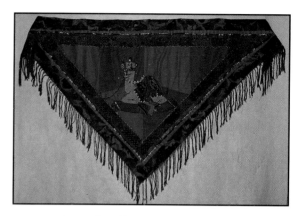

Large triangular fringed shawl with Kuwaiti camel applique. Designed and made by Annrae Roberts.

Body ornament or overlay, shown on dress, part of outfit "There's a Hot Time in the Old Town Tonight" by the author.

Detail of body ornament. Shown are the long streamers in front, interspersed with beads and tasseled at the ends. These streamers are attached to large diamonds of bodice, and hang free. Bottom row of bodice is shown in picture. On right side is necklace, made of smallest diamond (1" square) and fastened with hook and eye.

overlay specifically for the outfit "There's a Hot Time in the Old Town Tonight" for the Fairfield-Concord fashion show for their tenth anniversary. The overlay accents the plain short dress beautifully and carries out the colors of the coat lining, yet the overlay is equally workable with plain turtleneck jerseys and slacks. It's quite easy to do and here's how to do it.

You'll need assorted scraps: cotton, silk, satin, lamé, brocade, anything you like. I used three sizes of squares, 1", 1½", and 2½". These are finished sizes, which means you'll cut your squares ½" larger all the way around to include seam allowances. You'll need an equal number of squares for the lining or backing, and you'll need squares of thin batting for the filling.

Place a square of batting against the wrong side of a fabric square, then embellish it. You can stitch or quilt with any kind of thread and in any kind of pattern; you can add hand or machine embroidery; you can add beads or buttons, shi-shas or sequins, that's up to you. When this trimming is finished, place the square against the lining, right sides together, and stitch around three sides, like a little pillowcase. Trim seams if necessary, turn and finish the fourth side by hand. Both the front and back bodice sections are made up of nine of the biggest squares, sewn three across and three down. They are joined on point so they look like diamonds. Use the middle-size squares for shoulder straps, and mix the middle-size and small-size squares for streamers. These are also joined on point, sometimes with a bead or ribbon knot between, and each has a tassel on the end. There are six streamers, three for the front, and three for the back (see photo at left).

Margot Carter Blair used molas in two of her body ornaments. One, the larger one, is composed of the little round molas sometimes made by children learning the art. Margot unified these by choosing only molas which had bird designs, then outlined each one with a row of small wooden beads before she attached them to each other. This body ornament, like the one I just described to you, slips over the head.

Her second mola ornament is made of a larger medallion which is the focus of the design; it is almost more of a necklace than a body ornament. Small mola pieces joined together serve as the strap around the neck to hold it in place.

Margot calls the third ornament a flat tassel, and it was made to be worn with the black Othello coat, shown with it. It is all fabric. There is a yoke-like section across the back to which three fabric medallions are sewn; there are three more medallions below the yoke, and a couple more which hang from the center and support the streamer. All of the streamers are faced, and all are embellished with feathers and bells on the ends.

You don't have to have molas to make one of these, or use the same type of fabric medallion; there are many things which can be substituted and all you really need is the idea.

Elaine Zinn got her idea for the body ornament/ tabard from a photograph in a magazine, then designed her own. It is an ornamental tabard, or chasuble, as Elaine sometimes calls it. It can be worn over any number of plain outfits. Elaine chose Seminole patchwork as a design element and used it on both the front and back panels. These panels are the same size, about 6½" across the top where it fastens to the neckpiece, and about 16 or 17" across the bottom. Hers is ankle length, designed to be worn over pants or a long skirt. She used the neckline pattern from a dress as a guide for the neckpiece/collar. The back of the collar is in two sections, and closes with hooks and eyes so that it slips easily over the head.

Susan Jones' rainwear outfit (page 149) is filled with fantasy, although it has a practical side too. Susan reports that the raincoat material was quite expensive and she had a very limited quantity of it, so she used my Bog Coat pattern to make every inch count. The overlay is a collage of fabrics, including a paisley chintz from a challenge project. Susan used a fish design, a carp, and this also supplied her with the name of the outfit – "Stop Carping about the Weather." There is another carp on the back, and the whole overlay is abstract in shape and quite long in back. The outfit was a prizewinner at the AIQA fashion breakfast show in Houston in 1989.

Elaine Zinn wears "Indian Summer," her overlay/tabard decorated with Seminole patchwork.

Flat tassel, worn on black Othello coat, by Margot Carter Blair. Fabric medallions are embellished and joined together to create bodice, then attached to long faced streamers with feathered ends.

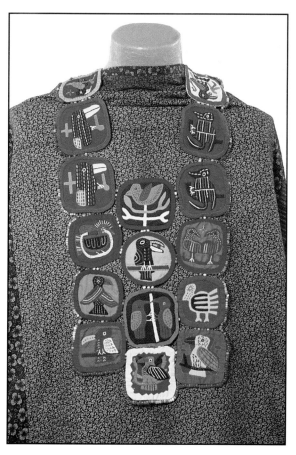

Mola overlay or body ornament by Margot Carter Blair. These small molas are joined together with an outline of painted wooden beads.

Another mola ornament or necklace, by Margot Carter Blair.

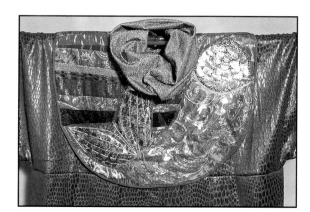

ABOVE: Front view of carp-decorated body ornament by Susan Jones. RIGHT: Back view of carp ornament shown over Bog-coat raincoat "Stop Carping about the Weather" by Susan Jones.

Neck-pieces and collars. The three on the left side are made of fabric scraps by the author; the neck-piece in the lower right hand corner was designed and made by Beryl Maddelena.

Three small envelope fabric bags. On the left, green wool challis pieced with antique Japanese obi silk, by the author. Yellow silk bag, pieced and embellished, designed and made by Ruth Stoneley. Aqua hand painted silk quilted bag designed, painted and made by Maria McCormick-Snyder.

Four bags by Beryl Maddelena, each with snap closures. Made of velvet, tapestry, silk and other luxury fabrics. Each is embellished with fabric flowers, buttons, pins with fake jewels, and fringe.

Big Mamma Tote by the author; a collage of brocade, tapestry, weaving, vinyl and laces. Body of bag made from 18" circles.

Crazy patch heart shaped neck pendants by Judith Montano, beaded and embroidered.

Victorian crazy patch bag, elaborately embroidered by Gerda Rasmussen. Collection of the author.

COLLARS AND BIBS

Collars and bibs are wonderful accessories and can change the whole look of a garment – and they also are fun and easy to make. Use the neckline facing pattern pieces from a dress or blouse pattern, pin the shoulder seams together, and trace the neckline. You can do anything you want to the lower edge, make it large or small, shaped, pointed or asymmetrical, but before you get too far with this project, cut a collar out of muslin or scrap material, using the neckline pattern, then try it on for fit. To vary the design, add a small Mandarin collar to the neckline, or outline the neckline with rows of covered cord in dog-collar fashion.

All of these collars or bibs need a thin layer of batting or Pellon® to give them some body. This is also true of belts and bags or purses, unless you are using very heavy fabric.

Collars or neckpieces take very little fabric, and you can also use up odd pieces of braids and ribbons for them; a purchased sequin motif or a fabric flower or two might be the starting point for a design.

BAGS, PURSES AND TOTES

No matter what name you give to it, a bag is absolutely indispensible. It holds the life-line supplies we carry around with us all the time, and desperately need! Bags, like our clothes and like us, come in all sizes and shapes, and most of us have quite a little collection of them – to go with different outfits and to carry for different occasions. Many are fairly easy to make; they can be tubes with round bottoms and drawstring loops, or they can be patterned after the ubiquitous envelope. They can be zippered pouches, clutches, or bags with snap closures. Look in the shops or boutiques, and look at the ads in fashion magazines and newspapers, and you'll get plenty of ideas. One company which specializes in patterns and supplies for any and all types of bags is Ghee's. They have frames, closures, chains, patterns and everything. You can get in touch with them at 106 East Kings Highway, Suite 205, Shreveport, Louisiana 71104 (318-868-1154), if you can't figure out how to make your own bags.

One of the bags pictured right is black silk, quilted in gold, with patchwork of plaid purple Thai silk. It is part of my outfit "Diamonds Are a Girl's Best Friend." The body of the bag is made of 7" circles, joined with a gathered straight grain gusset between the front and back circles. Following are the directions, so you can make your own version.

- Cut two paper circles 7" in diameter. Fold down the top of one circle to make a ¾" circle. This is the pattern for front and back of the purse. The full circle is the pattern for the flap.
- Using the three-quarter circle pattern, cut two of the outer fabric, two of the batting and two of the lining. Using the full circle paper pattern, cut two of outer fabric and one of the batting. Cut one strip of outer fabric 6" x 24". Cut the batting and lining the same. This is the gusset.
- Machine quilt through outer fabric and batting of front, back, flap and gusset; lay the wrong side of the lining against the batting of the gusset, and match the raw edges on both long sides together. Machine baste the long edges ¼" from the outer edge. Draw gathers up to fit the curved edges of the front and back sections. Stitch in place.
- Decorate or embellish the flap of the purse, working through the circle of outer fabric and batting. Place lining against the batting, and bind all outside edges. The flap will be attached by hand to the purse.
- Pin linings to front and back, right sides together, and stitch across straight edges. With the purse wrong side out, stitch across the gathered gusset ends. Turn the bag back to the right side, and hand finish the lining to the bottom edges of the front and back, covering the gusset seam. Add a wrist or shoulder strap, or carry as a clutch.

GATHERED BAG

Shown at right is a picture of a black-and-rust cotton bag and belt, part of the outfit "When Yo-Yos Last in the Dooryard Bloomed." This bag is also easy to make. There are only two sections of it, the front and back, and they are cut in a deep U, straight across the top. Both back and front were pieced and embel-

Black silk bag, pieced with purple plaid Thai silk, machine quilted in gold, by the author. Part of outfit "Diamonds Are a Girl's Best Friend." Instructions are included on this page.

Travel bag filled with compartments, made for the author by Rita Zerull. Guatemalan fabric and belts, needle-lace and tassels.

Purse and belt of black and rust cotton by Concord Fabrics, closely quilted in black and embellished with yo-yos. By the author.

GATHERED BAG

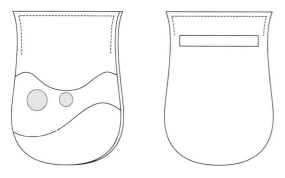

LEFT: Front with lining stitched across top and down sides. RIGHT: Casing in place on lining side of front and back. Long edges top-stitched and ends open.

A "bundle" or small bag of silk and Ultrasuede®, heavily beaded and embroidered, with decorated fringe. By Judith Montano.

lished and quilted, then joined together with the lining. The drawstrings are threaded through casings at the top of the bag, made by stitching through the outside and lining of the bag's front and back.

Because of the snap closing, this bag is assembled a little differently from the others. Place lining against the right side of the bag, both front and back sections, and stitch across the top and down each side (about 2½" from top on each side). Now turn the front and back sections and press the seam, then topstitch about ¼" from the seamed edge. Now you're ready for the casing.

Cut two strips of fabric on straight grain about 1" wider than the metal of the snap closure. These will be casing strips and they should stop about 1" or a little less from the outside edge of the front and back. Turn under the raw edges at each end, and stitch, then press under ¼" on each long side and pin the strips in place. This is the time to add a shoulder or wrist strap. Slip the ends of the strap underneath the edges of the casing strips, then stitch through all thicknesses.

You're ready now to join the front and back sections. Place them together, right sides facing, and stitch a close zigzag all around the edges, from one side opening to the other, then turn.

BIG MAMMA TOTE

Purses and bags come in all shapes and sizes, and one of the best big ones is the Big Mamma Tote. It's big enough to be a real tote and carry a lot of things, but it can be decorative enough to double as a purse. There are two pictured. The blue one, opposite page top, is of cotton designed by Shirley Botsford and was exhibited in her "Accessories as Art" show. It is based on 16" circles. The other, page 151 bottom, a rich collage of tapestry, velvet, vinyl and lace, is based on an 18" circle. I got the idea for the bag from Beryl Maddelena, who had a similar one. The handle or shoulder strap of Beryl's is cut in one with the body of the bag and thus goes up the center. The shoulder straps of mine are part of the side gusset, an extension of the gusset, and the bag fits close to the body. Instructions follow.

• Cut a paper circle the size of the body of the bag.

Cut a curved section from one side; this will be the bag opening. Cut two linings, two layers of batting, heavy Pellon® or fleece, and two foundation or base fabrics. Cover the base or foundation fabric with your fabric design and any embellishments you want to add. Put a pocket on the lining if desired.

- The gusset is about 4" wide and 2 yards long. You'll need one fabric strip for lining, one filler strip (batting or fleece, etc.), and one foundation strip which you will cover with pieced or collaged design. When outside gusset is finished, place it on top of lining strip with filler in between, and pin in place. Seam the ends of the outside-and-filler, separately, to form a circle. Repeat for lining. This seam will be at the bottom of the tote when the bag is assembled.

- Place back and front of bag on top of filler and lining, matching raw edges. Bind top opening curve of each. Baste layers together around outside edge. Pin one edge of gusset to outside edge of back, keeping gusset seam on the bottom of the bag. Now repeat for front. These seams will be on the outside of the bag, and all edges will be bound.

Big Mamma Tote, from Wamsutta® fabric designed by Shirley Botsford. Tote designed and made by the author.

BELTS

A walk through the belt department of any shop or boutique can give you an idea of the variety offered. As is the case with other accessories, it is limitless, and often, a striking belt can "make" a plain outfit. That one accent may be all you need. Many of the techniques offered in TRICKS AND TREATS work beautifully with belts, and you can get plenty of ideas from ads in magazines and newspapers too. I am including photos of some belts, and several of them are made from a pattern I devised for one of my workshops, and I'm passing it on to you (see pages 165-166).

This pattern is only for the belt front; you will have to add ties or a straight belt section for the back. Fold the paper pattern on the dotted line. This is the center front. Fold fabric for the outside, the lining, and filler (thin batt fleece or heavy Pellon®). Lay paper pattern on the fold of the fabric, and cut the three layers of the belt front. Place filler against wrong side of outside fabric, and sew the design through both layers.

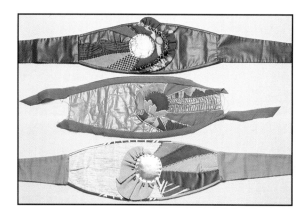

Three belts by the author. The one in the middle is in-progress to show assembly steps.

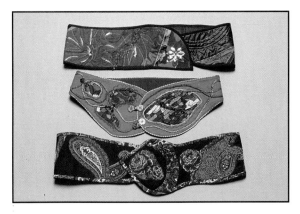

Three more belts. Top, by the author, of "wet and wrinkled" fabric, stitched and embellished, and fastened with a gold pin. Middle belt, of heavy green cotton by Mary Lu Stark. Closely stitched design of appliques; cords outline both top and bottom edges. Belt overlaps and fastens with antique gold button closures. Bottom belt of paisley cotton by the author.

Unfold the paper pattern for the design. It is somewhat fan shaped, with each section numbered to help in assembly. Do "spokes" one through five first, using a variety of fabrics. Stitch in place and decorate the seams. Add section 6 to cover the raw edges of the spokes, then complete the design with section 7. Section 7 can be fabric, couched cords, a pleated ruffle, or anything else that strikes your fancy. When all the decoration is finished on the belt front, place the lining behind it, matching raw edges, and pin in place. Bind the top and bottom edges of the belt front, add belt extension or ties, and fasten on the left side with a fancy buckle, a button, or Velcro®.

All accessories are designed to enhance and complement your outfit, whatever it may be. With a well stocked accessory wardrobe, you can change the look of you basic clothes at will. Often, an accessory may be more important than a garment.

CONCLUSION:
The last word

In the months since I began to pull this book together and get it in shape for the publisher, there have been catastrophic changes in our country, and in the world. Once again the threat of war, poverty and homelessness, disease, crime and escalating expenses threaten all of us. Both security and contentment are elusive. We have dropped slowly into an economic depression, and it takes most of our will and concentration to figure out how we can survive and surmount it.

We feel as though we are on a treadmill, going faster and faster all the time, and not getting anywhere. We juggle parenthood and jobs, struggling to solve personal, financial and emotional problems. Sometimes we think that if we work harder and longer we can make it O.K.; more often, we think we can't.

That old saying "All work and no play makes Jack

Jazz and sewing (and all the sister skills) are sisters under the skin, for in all, we are always improvising on a theme. The King Street Stompers: Joe, John, Gene, Wally, Fred, Kim, Pete, myself, and Harry.

a dull boy" was never more true. All work and no play makes Jill a dull woman. You must have a balance in your life, someway, somehow; you must take time to smell the flowers.

Sewing is one of the most creative and satisfying things you can do. It is also healing, and it can offer you the balance you need to counter the stress of daily living. You must take time for yourself, no matter what the pressures; in fact, the greater the pressure, the more essential it is for you to have a little time just for you.

Recently a long article about the revival of home sewing appeared in the *New York Times*. It mentioned that *Fortune* magazine predicted home sewing as one of the seven most promising industries for the future! It also mentioned, and I found this to be the most significant observation, that the return to sewing was not necessarily economic, but therapeutic. The article went on: "They (women) speak of a necessary counterbalance and creative stimulation in their lives, and of having a stylish wardrobe."

That's what this book is all about, as I've been telling you. The sewing is simple, and for the most part, only straight seaming is involved; also, the techniques are simple and basic and uncomplicated. The rewards are great, and so are the fringe benefits, for you are able to have unique, truly one-of-a-kind garments which celebrate you as a person. Believe me, it's a lot more fun to shop for fabric than to endure the frustration of shopping for ready-made clothes, and you have the excitement and challenge of creating something especially for you – with your colors, your design, your fabrics. Go for it!

TOP: Cartoon of the author's Dixieland jazz band, The King Street Stompers. CENTER: Poncho quilted with the cartoon. BOTTOM: Back view of jazz poncho. Cartoon by Pete Wells, poncho designed and made by the author.

PATTERNS

**BASIC GARMENT CUTOUTS FOR PAGE 9
(SHOWN FULL-SIZE)**

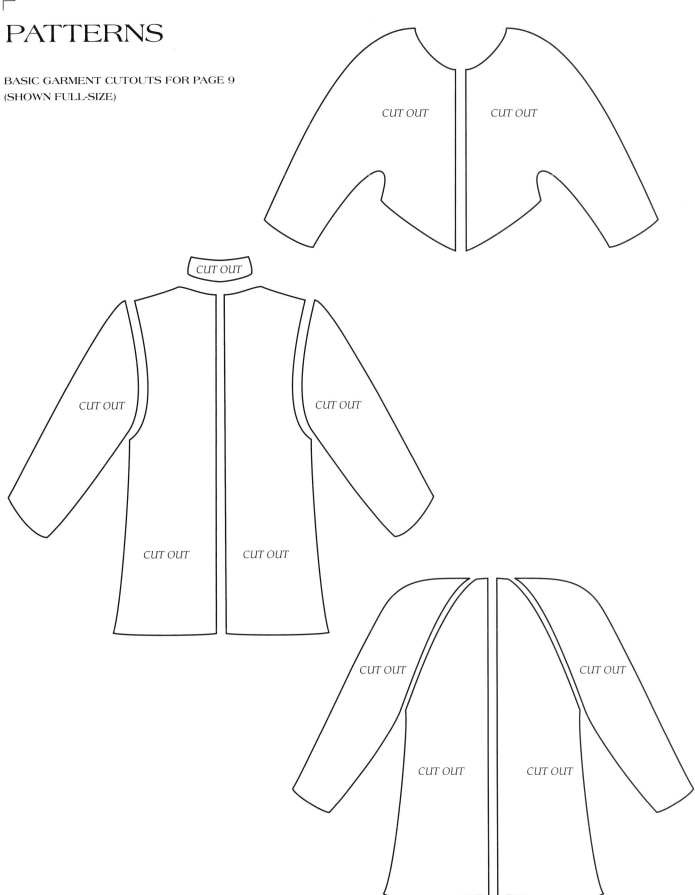

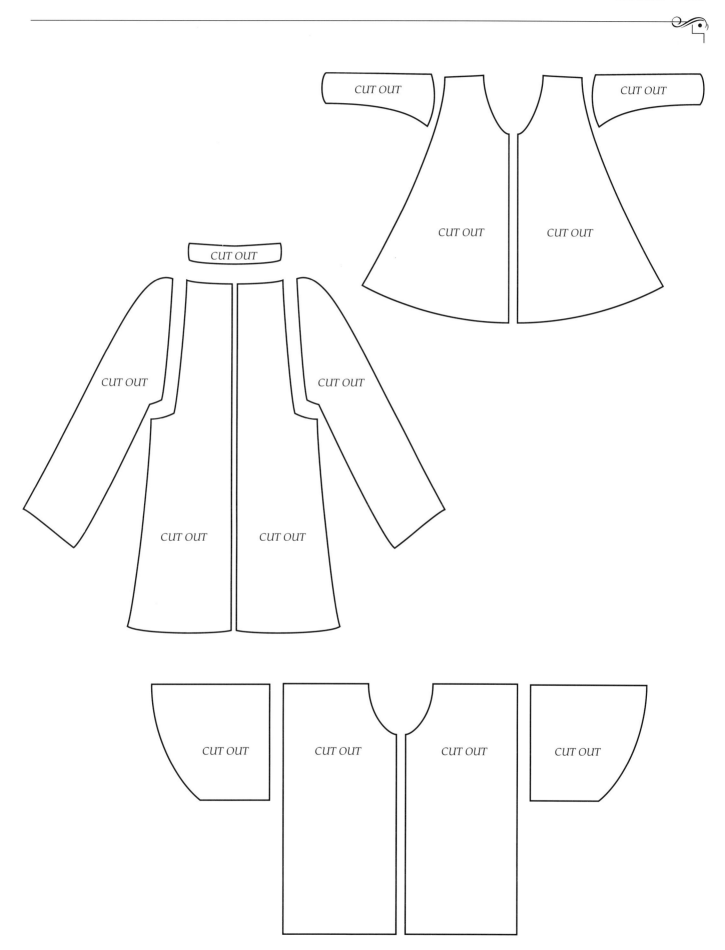

IN-SEAM POCKET PATTERN FOR PAGE 24
(SHOWN FULL-SIZE)

MANDARIN COLLAR PATTERN FOR PAGE 28
(SHOWN FULL-SIZE)

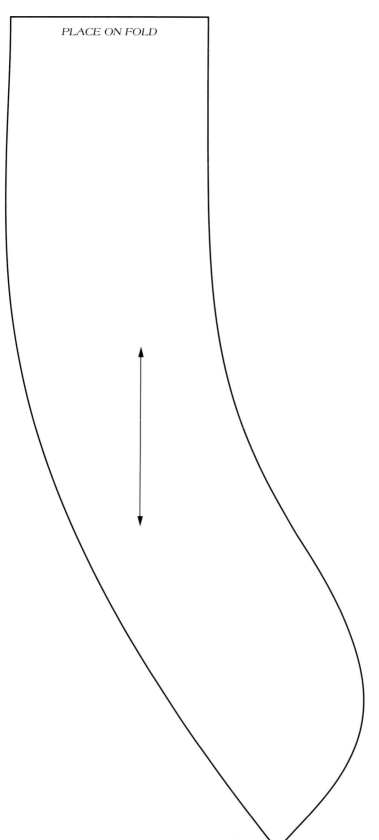

PLACE ON FOLD

FLOWER PATTERNS FOR PAGE 93-94
(SHOWN FULL-SIZE)

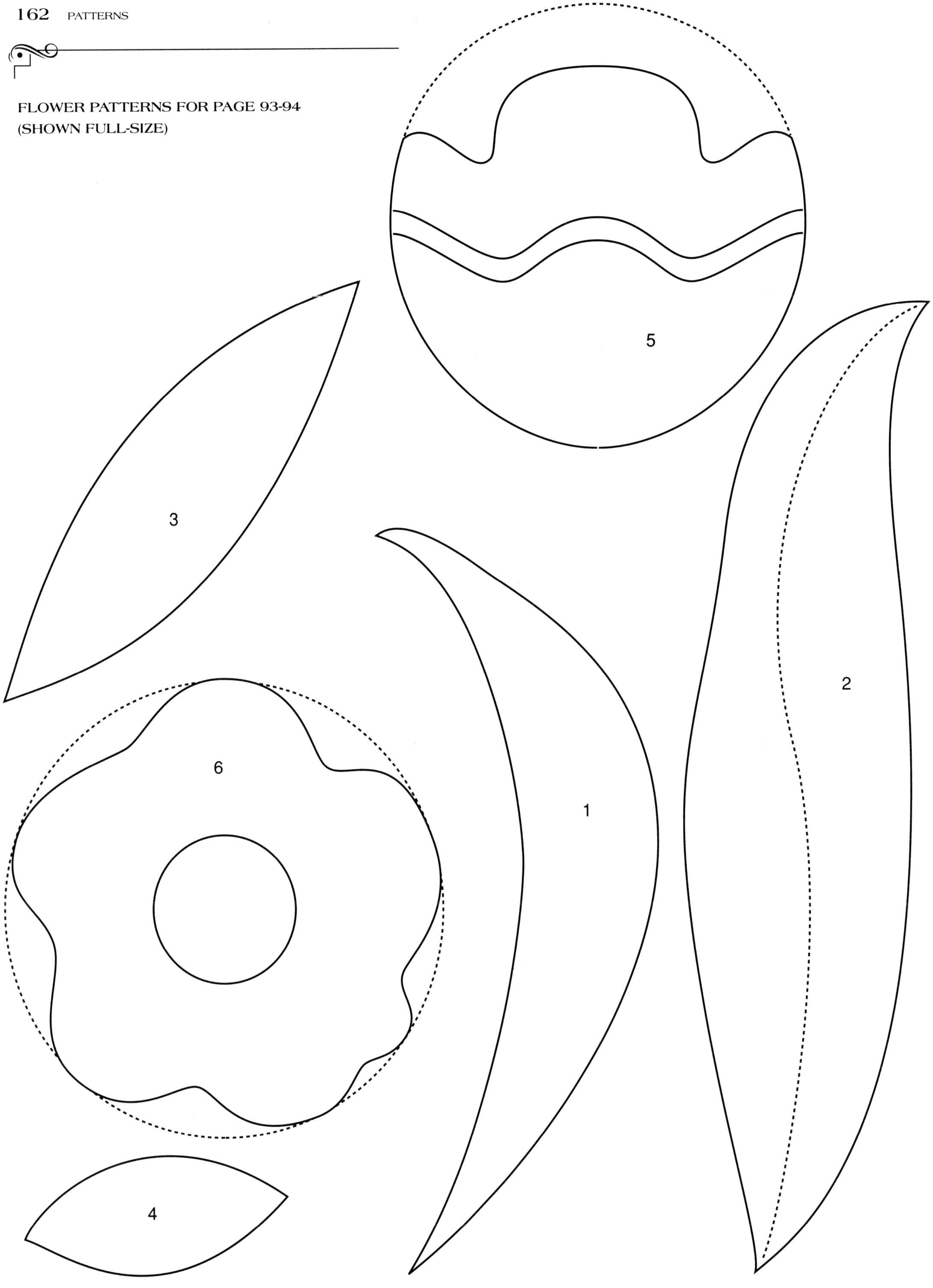

5

3

2

6

1

4

FLOWER PATTERNS FOR PAGE 93-94
(SHOWN FULL-SIZE)

FLOWER PATTERNS
FOR PAGE 93-94
(SHOWN FULL-SIZE)

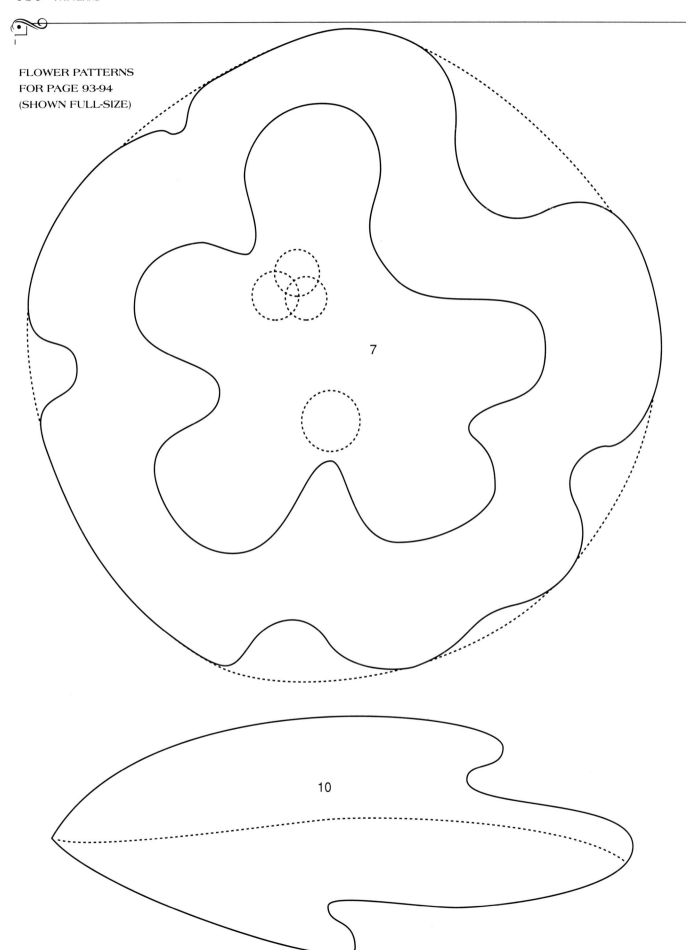

7

10

BELT PATTERN
FOR PAGE 155
(Pattern continued
on page 166

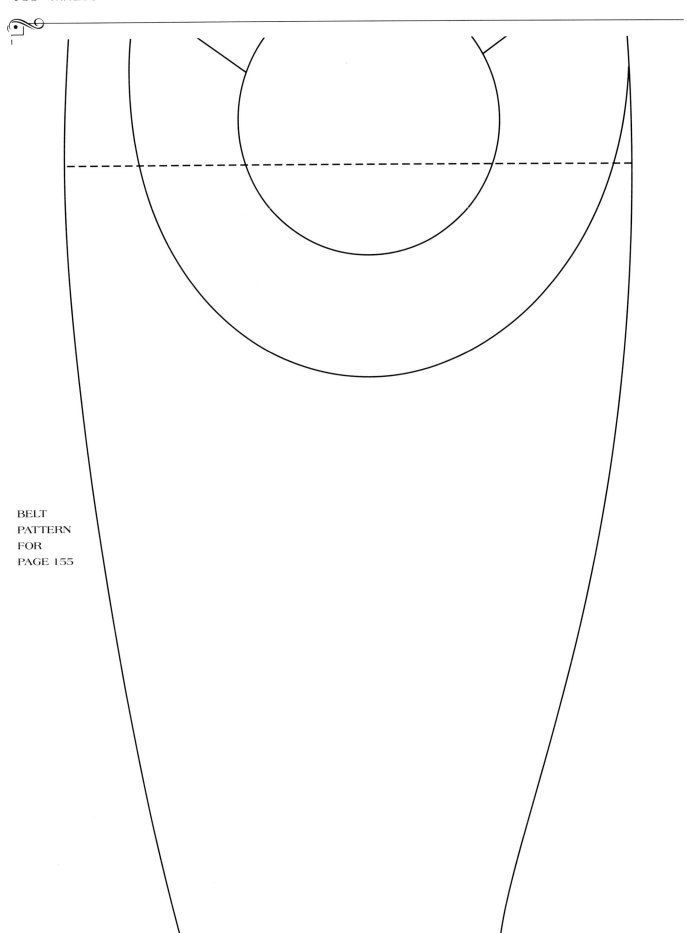

BELT
PATTERN
FOR
PAGE 155

∾American Quilter's Society∾

dedicated to publishing books for today's quilters

The following AQS publications are currently available:

• **American Beauties: Rose & Tulip Quilts**
by Gwen Marston & Joe Cunningham
#1907: AQS, 1988, 96 pages, softbound, $14.95

• **America's Pictorial Quilts** by Caron L. Mosey
#1662: AQS, 1985, 112 pages, hardbound, $19.95

• **Applique Designs: My Mother Taught Me to Sew**
by Faye Anderson
#2121: AQS, 1990, 80 pages, softbound, $12.95

• **Arkansas Quilts: Arkansas Warmth**
Arkansas Quilter's Guild, Inc.
#1908: AQS, 1987, 144 pages, hardbound, $24.95

• **The Art of Hand Applique** by Laura Lee Fritz
#2122: AQS, 1990, 80 pages, softbound, $14.95

• **...Ask Helen More About Quilting Designs** by Helen Squire
#2099: AQS, 1990, 54 pages, 17 x 11, spiral-bound, $14.95

• **Award-Winning Quilts & Their Makers:**
The Best of AQS Shows – 1985-1987 edited by Victoria Faoro
#2207: AQS, 1991, 232 pages, softbound, $19.95

• **Classic Basket Quilts** by Elizabeth Porter and Marianne Fons
#2208: AQS, 1991, 128 pages, softbound, $16.95

• **A Collection of Favorite Quilts** by Judy Florence
#2119 AQS, 1990, 136 pages, softbound, $18.95

• **Dear Helen, Can You Tell Me?**
...all about quilting designs by Helen Squire
#1820: AQS, 1987, 56 pages, 17 x 11, spiral-bound, $12.95

• **Dyeing & Overdyeing of Cotton Fabrics** by Judy Mercer Tescher
#2030: AQS, 1990, 54 pages, softbound, $9.95

• **Fun & Fancy Machine Quiltmaking** by Lois Smith
#1982: AQS, 1989, 144 pages, softbound, $19.95

• **Gallery of American Quilts: 1849-1988**
#1938: AQS, 1988, 128 pages, softbound, $19.95

• **Gallery of American Quilts 1860-1989: Book II**
#2129: AQS, 1990, 128 pages, softbound, $19.95

• **The Grand Finale: A Quilter's Guide to Finishing Projects**
by Linda Denner
#1924: AQS, 1988, 96 pages, softbound, $14.95

• **Heirloom Miniatures** by Tina M. Gravatt
#2097: AQS, 1990, 64 pages, softbound, $9.95

• **Home Study Course in Quiltmaking**
by Jeannie M. Spears
#2031: AQS, 1990, 240 pages, softbound, $19.95

• **The Ins and Outs: Perfecting the Quilting Stitch**
by Patricia J. Morris
#2120: AQS, 1990, 96 pages, softbound, $9.95

• **Irish Chain Quilts: A Workbook of Irish Chains & Related Patterns** by Joyce B. Peaden
#1906: AQS, 1988, 96 pages, softbound, $14.95

• **Marbling Fabrics for Quilts: A Guide for Learning & Teaching**
by Kathy Fawcett and Carol Shoaf
#2206: AQS, 1991, 72 pages, softbound, $12.95

• **Missouri Heritage Quilts** by Bettina Havig
#1718: AQS, 1986, 104 pages, softbound, $14.95

• **Nancy Crow: Quilts and Influences** by Nancy Crow
#1981: AQS, 1990, 256 pages, hardcover, $29.95

• **No Dragons on My Quilt** by Jean Ray Laury with
Ritva Laury and Lizabeth Laury
#2153: AQS, 1990, 52 pages, hardcover, $12.95

• **Oklahoma Heritage Quilts** Oklahoma Quilt Heritage Project
#2032: AQS, 1990, 144 pages, softbound, $19.95

• **QUILTS: The Permanent Collection – MAQS**
#2257: AQS, 1991, 100 pages, 10 x 6½, softbound, $9.95

• **Scarlet Ribbons: American Indian Technique for Today's Quilters**
by Helen Kelley
#1819: AQS, 1987, 104 pages, softbound, $15.95

• **Sets & Borders** by Gwen Marston and Joe Cunningham
#1821: AQS, 1987, 104 pages, softbound, $14.95

• **Somewhere in Between: Quilts and Quilters of Illinois**
by Rita Barrow Barber
#1790: AQS, 1986, 78 pages, softbound, $14.95

• **Stenciled Quilts for Christmas** by Marie Monteith Sturmer
#2098: AQS, 1990, 104 pages, softbound, $14.95

• **Texas Quilts – Texas Treasures** Texas Heritage Quilt Society
#1760: AQS, 1986, 160 pages, hardbound, $24.95

• **A Treasury of Quilting Designs** by Linda Goodmon Emery
#2029: AQS, 1990, 80 pages, 14 x 11, spiral-bound, $14.95

• **Wonderful Wearables: A Celebration of Creative Clothing**
by Virginia Avery
#2286: AQS, 1991, 168 pages, softbound, $24.95

These books can be found in local bookstores and quilt shops. If you are unable to locate a title in your area, you can order by mail from AQS, P.O. Box 3290, Paducah, KY 42002-3290. Please add $1 for the first book and 40¢ for each additional one to cover postage and handling.